Long Quiet Canadian Highway:
Waking Up In Canada

Martin Avery

Dedication: This non-fiction novel is dedicated to the marathoners at the 2013 Muskoka Novel Marathon as this novel was written during the Muskoka Novel Marathon in the summer of 2013. The writers: Martin Avery, Nora Bartlett, Nancy Beal, Noelle Bickle, Paula Boon, Sandra Clarke, Michael Codato, Cheryl Cooper, Kevin Craig, Carol Daize, Sherry Davis-Galvao, Connie DiPietro-Sparacino, Alison Doucette, Tobin Elliott, Lizann Flatt, Pat Flewwelling, Joanne Galbraith, M-E Girard, Alison Hall, Alyssa Hawn, Yvonne Hess, Emma Hogg, Dawn Huddlestone, Louise Hypher, Tara Laing, Tena Laing, Laura Litchfield, Paula Mazzocchi, Monika Moravan, Jacqui Morrison, Caroline Pattison, Brenna Pinckard, Dyoni Smith-Page, Brenda Storrie, Urve Tamberg, Lori Twining, Karen Wehrstein, Raphi Wehrstein, and Shellie Yaworski.

Long Quiet Canadian Highway: Waking Up In Canada

Martin Avery

"Every moment is enormous and it is all we have."
— Natalie Goldberg, Long Quiet Highway: Waking Up in America

"The air was soft, the stars so fine, the promise of every cobbled alley so great, that I thought I was in a dream."
- Jack Kerouac, *On the Road*

"When I wrote and got out of the way, writing did writing."
— Natalie Goldberg, Long Quiet Highway: Waking Up in America

On the road again
Goin' places that I've never been.
Seein' things that I may never see again
And I can't wait to get on the road again.
On the road again
-- Willie Nelson, On The Road Again

"Whether we know it or not, we transmit the presence of everyone we have ever known, as though by being in each other's presence we exchange our cells, pass on some of our life force, and then we go on carrying that other person in our body, not unlike springtime when certain plants in fields we walk through attach their seeds in the form of small burrs to our socks, our pants, our caps, as if to say, "Go on, take us with you, carry us to root in another place." This is how we survive long after we are dead. This is why it is important who we become, because we pass it on."
— Natalie Goldberg, Long Quiet Highway: Waking Up in America

"It is difficult to receive and accept oneness because human speculation doesn't catch it. But if you practice with full devotion, finally you will come to the final goal -- silence."
-- Katagiri, Each Moment Is the Universe

Those who manage to understand their destiny and the core of infinity begin to live happily, for they create the happiest infinity with their own thoughts.
—Anastasia

Table Of Contents

1. Waking Up In Ontario: An Introduction

After waking up in the Zen Forest, in the far east of Ontario, and at a Oneness event, west of Toronto, I felt I was in the Zen zone, so I did a tour of Central Ontario, teaching Zen Forest Meditation at yoga studios, et cetera, from Lake Ontario to Georgian Bay, from Belleville through Peterborough, Haliburton, Muskoka, and Parry Sound. I think of that region as Muskoka.

` I was a Reiki master, certified qigong instructor, and Zen meditation teacher, with a Diploma In Spiritual Healing from the International College of Holistic Studies. I was an energy healer, or qigong healer, and put together a program called Zen Power Hour, combining Zen meditation, Reiki massage, and qigong or energy exercises.

But then it came to an end.

I had a great time touring Central Ontario as a Zen teacher and healer.

Really, Muskoka is a district about a hundred miles north of Toronto that is about as big as Prince Edward Island. My Muskoka is much bigger and it includes everything from the Zen Forest, in the country north of Belleville, to Algonquin Park, and Georgian Bay to the Bruce Peninsula, as well as Owen Sound, the Blue Mountains, the longest freshwater beach in the world, Orillia, Lake Couchiching, and the Queen Elizabeth II Provincial Park, or QE2PP.

After that tour, I felt like returning to my old life as a high school teacher.

"Waking up" feels fantastic.

You know that feeling you get, sometimes, after peak experiences, such as hiking and climbing to the top of a mountain, skiing down a mountain, scoring the winning goal in overtime of a championship hockey game, or surviving a near death experience? The world glows, you feel connected to everything, and at one with the universe.

I've had that feeling lots of times, but it doesn't usually last very long.

After waking up in the Zen Forest and at the Oneness weekend, it lasted a long time.

Months.

And during that time, I traveled across Central

Ontario teaching Zen Forest Meditation, which combines Zen meditation with solo massage like Reiki self-healing massage and qigong or energy exercises. We called it Zen Power Hour. Sometimes we added past life work and future healing.

The hour-long workshops were a hit and I felt good about doing it as I knew I was giving people great tools to make their lives much better.

However, after a few months of living this dream, it ended.

Enlightenment is like that, they say.

There are different levels, according to Deepak Chopra.

Most people think that enlightenment is a state of ongoing bliss and oneness. They believe that after that, life is easy and simple forever after.

There is something called "the enlightenment experience" which has all of these characteristics, but the true enlightened life is something quite different.

The bliss is not the emotional experience we can know through the ego. It is beyond that.

My enlightenment experience was inspired by

two events.

First, the Zen master I had been working with for the past several years invited me to the Zen Forest for a special teaching session. He said he wanted to write a book. And by that, he meant that he wanted to talk while I took notes. He closed the Zen Forest for a week.

The only people in the place were the Zen Buddhist monk, two other monks who had trained in India, Korea, Japan, and Vietnam, and me.

We locked the gates.

Zen is sometimes called 'The Gateless Gate', but we locked the gates.

The monk meditated for an hour in the meditation hall he built for his retreat centre in the country north of Belleville, and then appeared, dressed in his best golden gown, and we met at the tea room on the bridge over the Zen Forest Pond.

He talked, I wrote.

I asked questions, he answered, and I wrote some more.

At the end of the day, I went over my notes and rewrote.

We did this day after day.

He said it would take a week to ten days.

"Maybe you will wake up, while working on this book," he said. "If you wake up while writing, we will take my name off the book and we will call you Zen master."

"If you don't wake up," he added, "we will throw the book into the Zen Forest Pond."

After a few days, the monk and Zen master said something that struck me as funny and I laughed long and hard.

He often said funny things and we shared a laugh.

There are a lot of stories, parables, and koans, in Zen, and my monk preferred the funny ones.

I cannot remember what he said that made me laugh so hard. It was something about reincarnation. He said, Nobody has died and come back to give us a full report about what death is like.

So, what about reincarnation? I said. Don't Buddhists believe in rebirth as an animal in the next life?

He often said things like, You are going to be a dog in the future. You might be come back as a tree. Or an insect living in a tree.

I asked him if the soul transmigrates into the body of another person or some animal. What is the difference between transmigration and reincarnation? Is it the same as rebirth?

He shook his head and said that is like asking, Is karma the same as fate?

These and a hundred similar questions are often put to me, he said.

A gross misunderstanding of about Buddhism exists today, he added, especially in the notion of reincarnation. The common misunderstanding is that a person has led a lot of previous lives, usually as an animal, and somehow in this life he or she is born as a human being. And in the next life, you will be reborn as an animal, or a deva in heaven, depending on the kind of life you lived.

This misunderstanding arises, he said, because people do not know how to read the sutras or sacred writings.

The Buddha left 84,000 teachings, they say. What that means is that the Buddha taught according to the mental and spiritual capacity of each individual. For simple village folks living during the time of the Buddha, reincarnation was a powerful moral lesson. Fear of birth into the animal world must have frightened many people from acting like animals in this life. If we take this teaching literally, today, we cannot understand it rationally.

It's a parable, he said.

Zen parables do not make sense to the modern mind, he added. If we learn to go beyond the parables and myths, we will be able to understand the truth.

Well than, I said, what is reincarnation.

He said, Reincarnation is not a simple physical birth of a person, like John being reborn as a cat in the next life. This notion of the transmigration of the soul definitely does not exist in Buddhism.

What Buddhism teaches is the ten realms of being.

At the top is Buddha and the scale descends as follows:

Bodhisattva, an enlightened being destined to be a Buddha, but purposely remaining on earth to teach others,

Pratyeka Buddha, a Buddha for himself,

Sravka, a direct disciple of Buddha,
Heavenly beings,
Human beings,
Asura, or fighting spirits,
Beasts,
Preta, or hungry ghosts, and
Depraved men, or hellish beings.
He had a lot to say about hungry ghosts.

"You don't want hungry ghosts to lick your lips!" he said.

These ten realms may be viewed as mental and spiritual states of mind, he said.

These states of mind are created by thoughts, actions, and words.

In other words, I said, these are not realms for reincarnation, they are psychological states.

Yes, he said. The realm of human beings has all the other nine states, from hell to Buddhahood. Man is capable of real selfishness, creating his own hell, or is truly compassionate, reflecting the compassion of Buddha.

In what realm do you now live? he asked me. If you are hungry for power, love, and self-recognition, you live in the Preta world, or hungry ghosts.

If you are motivated only by thirsts of the human organism, you are existing in the world of the beast.

I said, I often find myself surrounded by devas and feel like I'm in heaven.

Then you are in heaven, he said.

That made me smile.

But you have to remember to work on enlightenment, when you are in heaven, he said, or you will be reincarnated into one of the lower realms.

Ah, I said.

And for some unknown reason, that made me laugh, long and hard, until I woke up.

I told the monk, I think I can go home and finish this book now.

He smiled and nodded.

I went home and wrote faster than I ever had at a novel marathon and took it back to the monk the next day. That was a lot of driving and writing in a very short time.

While I was waiting for the monk to read the book, and comment on it, or throw it in the Zen

Forest Pond, I did some volunteer work at the Zen Forest.

The monk was building an outdoor eating area and my job was to level the ground for the surface. I had to pick stones and boulders, to clear the area, a rake and a hoe, to make it more or less level, and then a two-by-four to make it completely level.

The monk and Zen master came out to talk to me and saw me working.

He said, You now work like Zen master.

He said, You feel it is slow-going, but anyone watching you would see you working very fast. If you look at the clock, you will see you got a great deal done in a very short time.

Ah, I said. I see.

What about the book? I asked him.

He smiled and nodded.

My New Age guru, Janet Amare, went to India, to go to the Oneness University, and came back to Canada to spread the work about the couple who created the university and the movement. She is a natural healer, coach, author, intuitive channel, hypnotist, and expert in childhood and past life regression. I had taken several short courses with her, to become a Reiki master and qigong instructor, and so on, and studied with her for a year of weekends at the International College Of Holistic Studies to get a Diploma In Spiritual Healing.

She went to India after that and when she came back she invited me to a "mukhtu dishu", which was a long weekend of activities leading up to a Oneness Blessing.

For three days, we discussed spirituality, enlightenment, and what we wanted to manifest for our lives, we did qigong and danced, we fasted and put on white clothing, we brought in sacred objects to add to a big alter with icons and artifacts from many religions, including the Canadian religion -- hockey. The long weekend of activities climaxed with a blessing followed by savasanah, the yoga pose also known as the corpse position, which is usually done at the end of a yoga session.

The name comes from the Sanskrit words Shava, meaning "corpse", and Asana, meaning "posture" or "seat". It is also called the death pose.

Lying on your back, arms and legs spread at

about 45 degrees, as though you are on a cross, with your eyes closed, you breathe deeply and relax your whole body.

We were told to develop an awareness of the chest and abdomen rising and falling with each breath. All parts of the body were to be scanned for muscular tension of any kind, and it was consciously released with a small, repetitive, movement in the area.

All control of the breath, the mind, and the body is then released for about 30 minutes.

It is intended to rejuvenate body, mind, and spirit, we were told, as shavasana allows the body a chance to regroup and reset itself.

After yoga, the entire body will have been stretched, contracted, twisted and inverted.

After our three day workshop, our bodies, minds, spirits, and souls had been stretched, contracted, twisted, and inverted, and the corpse pose felt like a reward.

Shavasana gives the nervous system a chance to integrate that in what can be thought of as a brief pause before it is forced once again to deal with all the usual stresses of daily life, we were told, and after three days of working with a group, it was time for us to turn our awareness inward.

For three days, we heard more and more about a character called Bhagavan, who our guru had met in India.

Kalki Bhagavan was the title given to Vijay Kumar, an Indian spiritual guru. The title comes from traditional Hindu beliefs.

Kalki is the name given to the tenth incarnation of Vishnu, who will appear on a white horse, wielding a sword, Hindus say.

Bhagavan is a respectful form used to address spiritual teachers or guides.

Bhagavan's Oneness movement had used various names, including the Golden Age Foundation, Bhagavad Dharma, Kalki Dharma and the Oneness Organisation.

The movement started in a small school in Andhra Pradesh, India, and by 2008 it had more than 14 million followers worldwide.

Its stated mission is to "create oneness for all for lasting spiritual transformation".

The Oneness Temple, built at an estimated cost

of $75 million, had the largest pillar-less meditation hall in Asia.

Well-known visitors to the ashram included Bollywood stars, Rick Allen of Deff Leppard, and NBA coach Pat Riley.

Lying is savassanah at the end of the long weekend, I felt a sharp pain shoot up my leg, and then disappear, and I had a vision. I saw that light many people say they see during near death experiences, but I did not have to swim toward it. That light was right in front of me, just above me, almost in reach. Between me and that light there was a circle of people who were looking at me.

It was a great group of healers and holy men, some of whom I could not make out, as they appeared in silhouette in front of the light. Those I could see included Jesus, Buddha, Bodhidarma, Dr. Hsui, the Sai Baba, John of God, Adam Dreamhealer, the Dalai Lama, Thich Nhat Hanh and Thich Thong Tri, The Singing Rabbi, and a few others.

They guys I could not see well enough to identify looked like Native elders.

In case you never heard of all these people, let me explain:

Dr. Hsui, from Japan, gave Reiki to the world.

The Sai Baba was a great healer in India.

John of God was a great healer worked in South America.

Adam Dreamhealer was a young Canadian who was emerging as a very gifted healer.

Thich Nhat Hanh was the most famous Buddhist on the planet, after the Dalai Lama, the author of 100 books about Buddhism, including Jesus And Buddha Are Brothers.

Thich Tri Thong was my Buddhist monk and Zen master.

The Singing Rabbi was a rebbe I followed in my twenties. Shlomo Carlebach (שלמה קרליבך), known as Reb Shlomo to his followers (1925 – 1994), was a rabbi, religious teacher, composer, and singer who was known as "The Singing Rabbi" during his lifetime.

He told us he was the heir to a Chassidic dynasty but when we asked him which branch of Chassidism he belonged to, he said he was cooking up something new.

Although his roots lay in traditional Orthodox yeshivot, he branched out to create his own style combining Hasidic Judaism, warmth and personal interaction, public concerts, and song-filled synagogue services. At various times he lived in Manhattan, San Francisco, Toronto and Moshav Mevo Modi'im, Israel.

Carlebach is considered by many to be the foremost Jewish religious songwriter of the 20th century. In a career that spanned 40 years, he composed thousands of melodies and recorded more than 25 albums that continue to have widespread popularity and appeal. His influence also continues to this day in "Carlebach minyanim" and Jewish religious gatherings in many cities and remote pristine areas around the globe.

Carlebach was also considered a pioneer of the Baal teshuva movement ("returnees to Judaism"), encouraging disenchanted Jewish youth to re-embrace their heritage, using his special style of enlightened teaching, and his melodies, songs, and highly inspiring story telling.

He was descended from old rabbinical dynasties in pre-Holocaust Germany. He was born in 1925 in Berlin, where his father, Rabbi Hartwig Naftali Carlebach, was an Orthodox rabbi. The family left Germany in 1931 and lived in Baden bei Wien, Austria and by 1933 in Switzerland.

Some say Carlebach changed the expectations of the prayer experience from decorous and sombre to uplifting and ecstatic as he captivated generations with elemental melodies and stories of miraculous human saintliness, modesty and unselfishness.

During his lifetime, Carlebach was often relegated to pariah status, marginalized by many of his peers. Because in his yeshiva years he had excelled in Talmud studies, many had hoped that he would later become a Rosh Yeshiva or a similar figure; many harboured ill will toward his chosen path in music and outreach. In addition, his activities in public were often not considered proper according to traditional orthodox teachings. This included encouraging and listening to women singing (not relatives) and to show affection to them by kissing them, albeit in a fatherly manner.

In the years since his death, Carlebach's music has been embraced by many faiths as spiritual music. His music can be heard today in synagogues, Carlebach minyanim, churches, gospel choirs and temples worldwide. Many musical groups state that they draw inspiration from Carlebach and his music.

A musical written about his life, "Soul Doctor" received with critical acclaim.   A documentary film about Carlebach called "You Never Know," was released at the Jerusalem Film Festival.

Carlebach's approach towards kiruv (the popular Hebrew term for Orthodox Judaism outreach) was often tinged with controversy. Put most favorably, "He operated outside traditional Jewish structures in style and substance, and spoke about God and His love in a way that could make other rabbis uncomfortable."

Bodhidharma was a Buddhist monk who lived during the 5th/6th century CE. He is traditionally credited as the transmitter of Ch'an (Japanese: Zen) to China, and regarded as its first Chinese patriarch. According to Chinese legend, he also began the physical training of the Shaolin monks that led to the creation of Shaolinquan. He was father of Zen Buddhism.

Several stories about Bodhidharma have become popular legends, which are still being used in the Ch'an and Zen-tradition.

In Buddhist art, Bodhidharma is depicted as a rather ill-tempered, profusely bearded and wide-eyed barbarian. He is referred as "The Blue-Eyed Barbarian" in Chinese Zen texts.

Bodhidharma is said to have travelled to the northern Chinese kingdom of Wei to the Shaolin Monastery. After either being refused entry to the shaolin temple or being ejected after a short time, he lived in a nearby cave, where he faced a wall for nine years, not speaking for the entire time.

In one legend, Bodhidharma, they say, refused to resume teaching until his would-be student, Dazu Huike, who had kept vigil for weeks in the deep snow outside of the monastery, cut off his own left arm to demonstrate sincerity. In another version of the story, Bodhidharma told Huike he would not teach him until it rained red snow, so he cut his arm off and waved it around in the air over his head and the blood fell as red snow.

When I first arrived at the Zen Forest, the

monk and Zen master did a double-take when he saw me and said, Oh! You look so much like the Bodhidharma! Maybe you are the reincarnation of Bodhidharma!

I took it as a compliment, since he is famous for his strength and agility, for training the Shaolin monks, and for starting the martial arts like Judo, tai chi, et cetera, as well as taking Zen to China.

Later, I found out that Asian people consider him to be extremely ugly!

The message or meaning I got from that vision was easy to interpret but difficult to understand. I felt certain it meant that at that moment I could die or I could decide to go back to my life to work on enlightenment and help others reach enlightenment.

That sounded rather grand, I thought, but that's the message I got.

It was after those two 'awakening' moments that things came together so I could go on a tour of Central Ontario, teaching Zen Meditation, Zen Forest style, with massage like Reiki and energy exercises like qigong, plus some past life work and future healing exercises.

Just when it felt as though it was about to take off, and people were talking about me appearing in hockey arenas across the country, working with thousands of people, instead of yoga studios, working with dozens of people, I decided to stop.

I felt as though I was no longer in the Zen zone and it was time to go back to my old life, or something like it.

I looked around for a job, teaching high school in Ontario, which is what I had done for the past two dozen or so years.

There weren't many jobs for me to apply for in Ontario at that time, so I cast my net a little wider.

I got a great job offer from a university in China. A big university up north, where my childhood hero, Dr. Norman Bethune, had lived and worked, and where he died, and where there were many monuments erected in his honour, offered me a job teaching Canadian Literature and English. The university specialized in Engineering, but they also had a big Chinese Medicine department.

I might be able to study Chinese Medicine, there, while teaching English and CanLit.

The Spiritual Healing program was like an introduction to Chinese Medicine.

I accepted the position and started making plans to go to China.

However, I got an interesting job offer from a school in Canada, just then. It was a job teaching English and Drama in a French school in Northern Alberta.

It was a difficult decision to make.

I discussed it with the Zen master and the New Age guru.

The monk said he thought I should teach Zen meditation with him. An Easterner and a Westerner working together could reach a lot of people, he said. Also, he wanted to go on a trip to Vietnam and then follow a well-known hiking path through Cambodia to India, stopping to visit the Dalai Lama, and then up to Tibet, and back.

Or, he said, You should have a Zen relationship. Find someone for a Zen relationship and settle down, work less, and live in or close to the Zen Forest.

My New Age guru said, China has bad air and bad water, but it would be good for you to study Chinese medicine.

I decided to go for the Zen relationship and stay in Canada.

Someone I had met online an chatted with for a few years got a job in Edmonton at the same time I got a job offer from Cold Lake, about three and half hours north-east of Edmonton.

It felt like fate, something that was meant to be, so I said no to China and yes to Alberta. I went for it!

I would be working in a Catholic school in the oil patch between a military air force base and an air weapons range on the 55th parallel, which was a lot further north than the 45th parallel, where I was born and raised.

So, I woke up in Ontario and then decided to move to Northern Alberta.

I was a pacifist and an environmentalist, and my friends called me a New Age Zen Chri-Jew-Bhu. How would I do up north in the oil patch with jet fighter planes flying by in the sky all the time?

2. Waking Up In Alberta

I took a job in Northern Alberta, in a French school, which had become a Catholic school, in the Athabasca tar sands, in the City of Cold Lake, which had CFB Cold Lake on one side, a military air force base, and the Cold Lake Air Weapons Range on the other side of the biggest and coldest lake in Alberta.

What was a New Age Zen Christian Jewish Buddhist doing at a Catholic school in the Oil Patch? Besides teaching "army brats and oil patch kids" and I was living not too far from a cousin, my age, and her sister, a couple of years older, after a long time without seeing them.

I was writing and researching, exploring Northern Alberta, visiting Banff and the Rocky Mountains, again, and teaching English, Drama, and Creative Writing.

Despite the fact that Alberta is rather right wing, with lots of right wingers, conservatives, cowboys, rednecks driving pick-up trucks, and I was in a place that reminded me of the movie Avatar, I had a great time.

I had small classes in a new school where each student was given a MacBook as their personal laptop computer for school and my classroom had a Smartboard intead of a blackboard so anything I could get on my computer could be shown on the big screen, instead of notes written in chalk, which was the way we did it in Ontario.

My drama group won the provincial drama festival, held in Nordegg, in the Rocky Mountains. Directing a play in French was a real challenge. Teaching English in a French school was an interesting challenge. Working in a Catholic school was something else.

I was invited to teach Writing at Portage College, in Cold Lake, and I was invited to teach Zen meditation, Zen Forest style, with massage and qigong, at the Cold Lake Wellness Center and at Cold Lake's yoga studio.

Every weekend, I went to Edmonton, for the Zen relationship, and we had a good time getting to know the city and each other. The woman was a writer, a reporter, with a major daily newspaper, and I went with her on some of her assignments.

We went to murder scenes in Edmonton,

which her paper called Deadmonton, as it lead the nation in homicides, that year. We went up to Fort MacMurray to do stories on The Highway Of Death and the oil sands, or tar sands, the world's largest industrial development, or the biggest polluter on the planet, depending on your perspective.

I wrote a book of poetry called Celebrating Global Warming, stating "this is where we create and celebrate global warming". At Christmastime, I gave a copy of my book to all my colleagues, as a present.

The first year was a challenge, but the second year would be a lot easier, I was sure, since I knew my way around the school, the curriculum, the town, and half the province.

But then something horrible happened.

At the start of the new school year, while I was putting locks on lockers, for our students, I suddenly felt a huge stab of back pain, the kind that drops you to your knees, and I knew I had to get somebody to help me with it.

I did not have a doctor, as the waiting list for

doctors in Alberta was never-ending, and there was no walk-in clinic, and I was told the waiting time at the emergency department of the hospital was anywhere from three to six hours, so I thought about going to a chiropractor, for the first time in my life.

Both my brothers had back problems and one of them swore by chiropractors.

The other had back surgery to fuse his spine, in an attempt to end severe back pain, but it didn't work.

The first chiropractor I picked had a waiting list, so I went to the guy down the street.

He put me on his table and gave me an adjustment that took away my back pain right away.

However, over the next couple of weeks, I had trouble walking.

First I staggered a bit and then I walked like a drunk, or a spastic, unable to control my legs.

I went back to the chiropractor and he said, That happens sometimes.

He suggested going to the emergency department of the hospital.

The first doctor I saw said go home and have a hot bath and a shot of whiskey. He prescribed pain killers and anti-inflammatories, too.

My condition got worse.

The third doctor I saw sent me to the city to see an Emergency Neurology Specialist.

My cousins drove me down to the hospital.

By that time, I had spent three days with no legs. I dragged myself to the kitchen and bathroom and so on. After a few days, I could stand, so I was able to lurch around my place. And then I could take a step or two.

I could already walk a bit, and drive, when I saw the neurologist in Edmonton.

He took a look at me and saw a guy who could not walk, whose muscles appeared to be shutting down, and he decided I had GBS: Guillain-Barre Syndrome.

He said, Activate your short term and long term disability, get a doctor, and get ready for the worst. Twenty percent of people with GBS die. You might not be able to go back to work, or walk, again.

He set up a string of blood tests and nerve

tests, plus a spinal tap, and sent me on my way.

I laughed and he gave me hell for laughing, saying, This is very serious. You can't walk. You may never walk again. You could be dead in a short time.

I laughed some more and walked out.

A physiotherapist came to the same conclusion: GBS.

So, I found another physiotherapist.

I also found an alternative healer at a place called The Wellness Clinic. She said she was a reflexologist, but she did a lot more than any other reflexologist I had ever met. She had a gift for taking pain away.

The second physiotherapist I found also did acupuncture.

With the help of the reflexologist and the physiotherapist who did acupuncture, I healed myself, using everything I had learned in the Diploma In Spiritual Healing course, in which I had become a Reiki master, and using everything I learned from the Zen master, including meditation, massage, and energy exercises, or qigong.

I was off work for several months but made a return in the spring. That was amazingly fast, the benefits group told me.

I don't think you're coming back, the principal of my school said.

I showed her the doctor's note saying I could go back to work, along with reports from the neurologist and the physiotherapist.

The director of our school board told the principal that they had to follow the doctor's orders, so I went back to work half-time for a couple of weeks and then full-time.

It was a long journey but I celebrated every step. I was ecstatic when I could stand, again, take a few steps, when I got a walker to help me get around, when I graduated to canes, and when I got rid of the canes.

I spent a lot of time in the swimming pool on the air force base and in the gym at the town's rec centre, called The Energy Centre.

And my students and colleagues, the other teachers, celebrated my return with me.

And just when I thought I had my old life back, the principal pulled the rug out from under my feet, as they say. She told me my contract would not be renewed.

Another teacher's contract was not renewed, two teachers were transferred, one quit, educational assistants were fired, and students started transferring to other schools.

It became apparent that the high school half of our K to 12 school would be closing.

Almost all the teachers were chased away and the others saw the writing on the wall so they started looking for new jobs, too.

It was a very sad way to end the school year.

I applied for teaching jobs in Alberta and the Yukon as well as Ontario and China, the U.K., and the U.S.A.

While I was waiting to hear from them, I went on a little trip, after the school year ended, to say "So long" to Alberta. First I drove down to Edmonton and Calgary, then up to Banff and Jasper, and then I went to Lac La Biche to say "So long" to my cousins. And then I decided to go back home to Ontario for a while.

I gave away most of my belongings and hit the road. I decided to drive from Cold Lake, in

Northern Alberta, on the 55th parallel, down to my old hometown, in Muskoka, or Central Ontario, on the 45th.

But what would I do if I couldn't find another teaching job?

The second last day of work, at school, I sat and marked, recorded marks, finished report cards, interrupted by students dropping by to say "So long," "Thanks for being an awesome techer," "I'm not coming back to this school, since they chased away so many good teachers," and the little kids cried, and the big kids swore, and a few of the teachers and EAs also came through my doorway, to cry or swear.

I completed an inventory of books in the English collection.

One of the angriest, most injured, most unhappy teachers came to my room to count down the final minutes until quitting time.

As I pulled out of the parking lot at school, CBC Edmonton played k.d. laing's version of the Leonard Cohen song, Hallelujah, and I sang along as I drove up north to see the lake, in all its natural beauty, and then went home to bed, after eating a toasted roast eef sandwich, vowing I'd be a vegetarian again, soon.

I felt exhausted.

After snoozing for an hour, I put on my new hiking shorts and a matching shirt and ball cap, drove up to Cold Lake Provincial Park, and hiked the hilly trail beside the lake: It took ten minutes to reach a bench and after a ten minute rest I hiked another fifteen minutes to a picnic table, where I could sit and write.

It was sunny, 25 degrees, the heat felt great, and a brisk breeze off the lake felt good, sounded great, and kept the bugs away.

I had no idea what would happen next in my life. I was unemployed. Or retired.

I had a lot ideas about what I wanted to do, and other things I might do, but it was all wide open, with nothing lined up.

I had applied for teaching jobs in Scotland, England, the U.S.a, Ontario, and Alberta, but I'd heard nothing in response. Absolutely nothing.

Well, the U.S.A. said they wanted me for the VIF program the next year.

The Visiting International Faculty program took teachers from other countries and sent them to place in the U.S. that did not get a lot of international visitors.

Did I want to spend a couple of years working with hillbillies and rednecks in the sticks, somewhere in the Ozarks or rural Florida?

Hell, yes!

I was skipping the final dinner party for work, since I'd been fired, or let go, or my contract was not renewed, or chased out, like all the other high school teachers at my school.

They said they wanted me to go to the year-end party, but that made no sense to me.

I know you are supposed to go to farewell parties for the other people, nto for yourself, but I had been let go and I did not feel like going to a party. I wanted to be there for the teachers and EAs who had been fired, got transferred, or quit, or had to go back to teaching elementary school, or whatever. But not on that night.

The high school was dying.

The phys ed guy called the school The Titanic.

Teachers were chased away and the students ran away to other schools. The principal blamed the teachers. The teachers, students, parents, other stoff, blamed the principal, or the director. Some said it was just politics and the real problem was higher up.

I lost interest in their games and issues. I felt happy I was able to get two years in, had a good time, got paid, and was getting out.

A colleague, from France, also fired, said,We have been given a gift that did not look like a gift when we got it but turns out to be much better than what we wanted, which was to stay on the Titanic.

It's like the Statue of Liberty, I said, a gift from France to the U.S.A., and he said, Yes!

He was planning to go back to France, after stopping in Montreal, and he wanted to walk the Camino, the spiritual walking trail that crossed Spain and France. -- He wanted to do the French part.

The Titanic never made it all the way across the Atlantic, to the Statue of Liberty, he said.

I had half a mind to jump in my car, drive across Canada, and get my old life back.

But you need your whole mind to drive across the Prairies and Northern Ontario, especially on the Canada, July 1st to July 4th weekend, when drivers from the U.S.A. and across Canada would clog the Trans-Canada Highway and there would be record numbers of drinking and driving accidents.

I had been trying to manifest a job and a move to the mountains, to teach and live in Canmore, and hang out in Banff, so I could explore the Rocky Mountains.

I wanted to launch the Banff Zen Centre, develop it into an integrated healing arts centre, franchise it, and then sell th whole thing, so I could heal the world in the time of global warming.

I wanted to move mountains. But I was in rough shape, so I thought I'd start by hiking in the mountains.

I contemplated riving over to Jasper and down

the Icefields Parkway to Banff, Lake Louise, and Canmore, for a couple of weeks of mountain climbing.

But Banff, Canmore, Calgary, and that whole Kananaskis area had been hit hard by rain and glacial meltwater and floods, recently, and was still recovering.

So I decided to head home.

Three days later, I would be sitting at a picnic table by a river in Muskoka, writing my memoirs, with the hot sun tanning my back.

The best way to say good-bye to Alberta, I'd say, is to go to Banff or Jasper, spend the night, wake up in the Rocky Mountains, Canadian edition, and spend a day on the Icefields Parkway.

The Icefields Parkway, or, as they say in French, Promenade des Glaciers, also known as Highway 93 north, how poetic is that? is an incredibly scenic road in Alberta, that parallels the Continental Divide, traversing the rugged landscape of the Canadian Rockies, travelling through Banff National Park and Jasper National Park, linking Lake Louise with Jasper and connecting with Highway which goes west to Yoho National Park in British Columbia and east to Banff.

The Bow Valley Parkway also links Lake Louise and Banff, and it's beautiful, but not many roads or routes or highways can compete with the Icefields Parkway.

The Icefields Parkway, 230 km (140 mi) long, is named for the Columbia Icefield, visible from the parkway.

In July and August the I.P. sees up to 100,000 vehicles a month.

The parkway is two lanes with occasional passing lanes. The Parkway minimizes grades and hairpin turns but travellers must look out for wildlife and for vehicles stopped on the shoulder, as well as rubber-neckers.

Snow can be expected at any time of year and extreme weather is common in winter.

A Canadian national parks permit is required to travel on the Icefields Parkway; stations near Lake Louise and Jasper enforce the law.

Commercial trucks are prohibited.

The speed limit is 90 km/h (55 mph) and the

limit is reduced at Saskatchewan River Crossing and the Columbia Icefield area.

In winter, chains or all-season radial tires are required by law and road closures are not common.

Going northwest from Lake Louise, the Icefields Parkway passes Crowfoot Glacier, Bow Summit, Peyto Lake, Mistaya Canyon, Saskatchewan River Crossing, Parker Ridge, Columbia Icefield or Athabasca Glacier, Icefield Centre, Athabasca Falls, Sunwapta Pass and Sunwapta Falls.

Campgrounds spot the length of the Parkway and provide water and firewood.

The Parkway is easily cycled between Banff and Jasper over three to five days and self-supported riders are common in summer. Bicycle tour operators also use the Parkway, often extending the ride to five days to leave time to drive back to the start.

A friend of mine, a woman who lives in Canmore and works in Banff, was chatting with me online when the flood hit. First she said the little creek that runs through Canmore was rising and she was thinking about taking out her kayak. She had planned a midnight mountain bike ride on the night of the super moon but canceled it because of rain and floods. Later she texted me to say she just saw a refrigerator floating down the raging river where her little creek had been. Not long after, she said there was a house following the refrigerator down the river.

My New Age guru sent me her newsletter. It said there would be a lot of portals open in June, so you might notice a lot of people dying, many babies being born, and lots of people you know making big, life-changing, decisions.

That resonated with me and with my experience. My school was dying and all the high school teachers were looking for new jobs.

She said that July would be a good time to rest and re-group.

That sounded good to me.

I decided to go back to Ontario, where it was warmer, and there were great lakes for swimming around my old hometown, in Muskoka, and the Zen Forest, as well as the novel marathon.

And she said that in the autumn, there would

be new energy and new opportunities. She said that it would be a time when things that had appeared to be impossible or even unimaginable would become your new reality.

I tried to imagine what was unimaginable for me.

What would my new life be like. After a hot summer of swimming and writing, resting and regrouping, I would have to be ready for the formerly impossible and unimaginable.

3. Waking Up In Cold Lake

After two years at the school in Northern Alberta, I left, along with almost all the other high school teachers, as the "secondaire" side of the school was closing due to declining enrolment. We didn't like the way the closing of the high school was handled, but that's another story, for another book.

At the end of the school year, at the end of June, I took a couple of weeks to get ready to leave, and then I drove back to the Zen Forest.

It's a simple trip: You follow the Trans-Canada Highway to Sudbury, and then turn south.

I would be going from the 55th parallel of latitude to the 45th, from Cold Lake, Alberta, to Coldwater, Ontario, from my new home to my old hometown, from the past to the future.

My plan was to drive across Saskatchewan, Manitoba, and Northern Ontario, to Huntsville, in time for the Muskoka Novel Marathon, and then visit my brother, in Midland, go to a reunion in my old hometown in Muskoka, go canoeing for a few days with a friend, go kayaking with my brother in Georgian Bay, and then head for the Zen Forest.

I planned to move to Belleville, the closest city to the Zen Forest, a small city, a slow city, to go to Loyalist College, to take a post-graduate course in Public Relations, so I could change careers, go back to my first career, and do that for a decade or so before I retired, again.

I retired at age 50, but I didn't like it, so I went back to teaching, again.

My retirement last about two months, or one summer. I realized I loved teaching high school and missed it.

A friend said I was addicted to teaching and the school year, I was a recovering high school English teacher, and I needed a twelve step program. But he was just joking around. I think.

In short, I planned to drive from Cold Lake, in Northern Alberta, across Saskatchewan and Manitoba, to Huntsville, Muskoka, in Central Ontario, in time for the Muskoka Novel Marathon. And when I got there, I planned to write a book about the trip across Canada, and I planned to call it Long Quiet Canadian Highway: Waking Up In Canada.

It was a big allusion to Natalie Goldberg's

book, Long Quiet Highway: Waking Up In America. And I contemplated driving through Minnesota, on my way home, to visit the Minneapolis Zen Center, where Goldberg studied Zen, and which she writes about in Long Quiet Highway and some of her other books.

But I was a Canadian nationalist, loved Canada, and wanted to travel through Canada, instead of the U.S.A., even though MapQuest and Google Maps said it was a little shorter to cut through North Dakota and Minnesota than to drive through Northern Ontario. It was better to go under Lake Superior than over.

I had traveled across Canada several times and take the route that follows the north side of Lake Superior a dozen times. It was long and quiet but I liked it.

And Lake Superior had changed, with global warming, I had heard; you could now swim in the huge lake, as it had warmed up a good deal. -- I wanted to try that!

So, as I planned to start my trip, I was of two minds about the route: Should I cut through the U.S.A., or keep it strictly Canadian?

The Canadian part of me wanted to drive across Northern Ontario.

The Zen part of me wanted to visit the Minneapolis Zen Center in Minnesota.

A couple of days before I left Cold Lake, I drove over to Lac La Biche, to visit my cousins, and say "So long". I gave them a carload of furniture plus a couple of bags of clothes and some sports equipment: hockey skates, cross country skis with boots and poles, never used.

I took my cousin over to Winston Churchill Park so we could walk along the beach and wade in the water of Lac La Biche. We had a good talk and said our goodbyes.

At her sister's house, my other cousin's daughter and her daughter were in town, and they had just picked up their dog, from the airport, as it had flown from New Zealand to Vancouver and then up to Edmonton.

It was a barky little girl called Charlie and its owners were surprised that she and I hit it off almost right away.

"Usually, she barks at men," Kezia said.

"Especially big guys with beards, wearing ball caps."

"A lot of dogs are like that," I said.

"But you've got that whole Zen thing going on," she said.

That made me laugh.

After a couple of years at a French Catholic school in Northern Alberta, in the oil patch, beside the air force base and air weapons range, I still had the Zen thing going on, she said.

My cousin asked me how I was going to drive across the country. "Through the U.S., or stay in Canada?" she said. "And how can you do it alone, without anyone to talk to? Do you listen to the radio or c.d.s or talking books, or what?"

I told her I meditated, while driving, and that made her laugh.

How can you drive while meditating? she said.

You can meditate while doing anything and everything, I said.

Driving?! she said.

The Zen monk taught me how, I said. He showed me the magic, secret, method.

Yeah, right, she said.

My cousin is very smart. She was identified as gifted, as a kid in school, and it is hard to pull the wool over her eyes and get her to believe anything she thinks cannot be true.

You can meditate while doing anything and everything, I told her. The Zen monk taught me how to meditate all day long. It's like praying incessantly, in a way.

Her sister was quite religious, and she was very close to her sister, so she understood that, she said.

Driving across Canada, twelve or thirteen hours per day, for a few days, or just eight hours a day, for four days, would pass by like a few minutes, or nothing, if I meditated while driving.

My plan was to drive across a big chunk of Canada in three or four days, stopping at the Minnesota Zen Centre, possibly, and arriving in Ontario in time for the Muskoka Novel Marathon.

After a driving marathon, I would do the novel marathon.

I planned to write a book about my trip across

Canada and call it Long Quiet Canadian Highway: Waking Up In Canada.

It would be an hommage and an allusion to A Long Quiet Highway by Natalie Goldberg.

I really liked Natalie Goldberg.

Long Quiet Highway begins with stories from her childhood, about growing up in a Jewish family in New York. Her book follows the path that she took to find the true meaning of her life through writing and Zen Buddhist practice.

The book is broken up into five sections.

In the first section she focuses on her childhood experiences that shaped her life.

She describes herself as a dork.

The main focus of this book, in a way, is how to write. Writing is her life and she realized, with the help of her Zen master, that writing, like life, is something you just have to keep trying even if you do not feel like it or you want to quit because you are not successful.

She asks the question, What is success, anyway? "

Success is none of our business, she writes. It comes from outside, and therefore is no concern of ours.

In other words, you will not be truly successful if you are so concerned with success. More importantly, whether you get external, or professional recognition, or not, is ultimately unrelated to the writing life.

The third part of Long Quiet Highway tells the story of the author's budding relationship with Zen coinciding with her marriage and her move to Minnesota. She expresses her frustrations and trials with trying to be a good Zen student, even when her marriage is falling apart.

The study of Zen became the focus in her life.

Part four explains how it felt for her to leave the harsh winters of Minnesota and return to New Mexico. She describes her struggle trying to write and being without her Zen master.

She had to learn to live without him, especially when he was diagnosed and eventually dies of cancer. His death was a test of Zen learning.

Natalie Goldberg writes about moving on after her master's death, in the fifth part of the book.

She uses her writing as therapy, as memoir, as a gift, and in the end she accepts her role as a teacher to all sentient beings and herself.

I've written about growing up in Muskoka, in other books, and about how much I loved going to Bracebridge and Muskoka Lakes Secondary School, loved the University of Victoria, the Banff Centre School of Fine Arts, York University, New College Writers Workshop, the University of Toronto, Vermont College of Norwhich University, not as much, Queen's University at Herstmonceux Castle in England, and the Stratford Campus of UT/OISE.

Unlike Goldberg, I did not have a Jewish childhood. But I had a Jewish decade, when I was in my twenties and lived in Toronto, with a year in Jerusalem. After that, I had a New Age decade and then a Zen Buddhist decade.

And I had just finished two years at a Catholic school, as a teacher. I was ready to leave the harsh winters of Northern Alberta for the soft winters of Southern Ontario.

Writing has never been a struggle, for me; it has always been a joy. I enjoyed early success, followed by years of anonymity as an author, but lots of fun as a freelance journalist and sports columnist, a biographer and memoirist. After I woke up in the Zen Forest, I wrote and published a lot of books quickly, working like a Zen master, as my Zen master would say. At last count, I had 90 books in print. My goal was hit a hundred and compete with Balzac. And after that, I planned to write another hundred books. I wanted to keep writing until I was in my eighties, like Alice Munro.

My Zen master almost died of a heart attack, a few years ago, but we talked him into having a heart by-pass operation, so he was still alive and well and working in the Zen Forest. I was looking forward to seeing him and working with him again.

He wanted me to teach Zen meditation with him, and to go on a walking tour of Zen Buddhist places, from Vietnam to Tibet, by way of India, with him.

I wasn't sure about that!

I wanted a Zen relationship with a woman and decades of living happily ever after.

I did not use my writing as therapy, but I used it as memoir, and thought of it as a great gift. I loved my role as a teacher to, as they say, all sentient beings and myself.

Don't just do something, we say; sit there.

Everybody else says, Don't just sit there, do something.

Zen is all about sitting practice.

But today is all about moving.

As I pack up my belongings for another move, I discovered several manuscripts for books. I've been counting my books as I was getting close to 100.

Balzac wrote 100 books in a series called The Human Comedy. Ever since I won the Balzac Prize for Poetry, I've been competing with Balzac, writing a 100 book series called The Human Comedy.

At last count, I was at 90. I posted it on my Facebook page.

But today, while getting ready to move, I found:

America United 9/11

Water Wars

Metamorphasis

The Republic Of Ontario

Who Killed Canada
and some others.
Murder On The Bruce
The Silkey Hunt
a book about writing
a novel I can't find a title for

And that, ladies and gentlemen, makes 99 books.
So this book, Long Quiet Canadian Highway,
is #100.
Let's celebrate!

But then I found a few more:
My Mayan Romance
How To Make Love Stay
So Long, Lizard Brain

It turns out I am already past the 100 book mark!
Take that, Balzac!
Now, to take aim at 200 ....
If I keep writing for another couple of decades,
like Alice Munro, that would mean ten books a
year, or less, not even a book a month. -- No
problem!

Judging by the titles, topics, and my memories of the contents, I think it is safe to say I was not a happy camper, back in the day, when I wrote those books. war, murder, hunting, right wingers, terrorists, love leaving, and the lizard brain. -- oh my!

Good thing I took myself to that Zen retreat!

Well, a lot of things happened after those days, when I wrote those books.

I was living in Owen Sound and following the men's movement, led by Robert Bly. I did a long weekend workshop with Bly at Trent U. in Peterborough. After that, I got married, divorced, moved back to my old hometown, was happy there for half a decade, moved again, then went to the Zen Forest.

And now I can feel the pull of my old hometown, once again. Or the home region. Muskoka has a magnetic pull, an electro-magnetic attraction, a tractor beam stronger than any on Star Trek. I could feel it when I left and now I can feel it drawing me back across the prairie and around

Lake Superior like the homing instinct of a great migrating bird, like a raven returning to Gravenhurst, or the pelicans flying from Cold Lake to the Gulf of Mexico, or snowboards leaving Florida for their summer homes in Muskoka.

If a trip across Canada sounds like a wild and crazy adventure through forest, wilderness, or muskeg, with bears and other wild animals, well, MapQuest.ca makes it sound .... different.

Total Travel Estimate: 3241.72 kilometres - about 37 hours 53 minutes.

Google Maps was less, um, poetic, and suggested I could do it in three days, driving to Winnipeg the first day, Wawa the second day, traveling 13 hours at 100 kmh, covering 1300 km per day. That would put me in Midland in three days.

Google Maps said the trip from Alberta to Ontario, through the Northern USA, along US-2 E, was 3,143 km, and would take 34 hours, but the all-Canadian route, along the Trans-Canada Hwy E, was 3,308 km, and would take 34 hours. It was a couple of hundred km longer, but it would take about the same time.

In Canada, we measure distance by time, rather than miles or kilometres.

Adding a stop at the Minnesota Zen Centre would add one hour to my trip.

Should I do it?

Did I want to write a book about waking up in Canada, or waking up in the U.S.A.?

I decided to sleep on it.

When and where would I wake up?

4. Waking Up In Saskatchewan

In the morning, I woke up thinking that what I really wanted to do was see Northern Ontario, again. I was looking forward to seeing Saskatoon, Regina, Brandon, Winnipeg, Kenora, Thunder Bay, Wawa, Sault Ste. Marie, and Sudbury, again. I was long forward to the long, quiet, Canadian highway that linked all those places together.

I could go to the Minnesota Zen Center some other time.

I could go to the Rochester Zen Center, on the other side of Lake Ontario from Belleville and the Zen Forest, when I got back to Ontario.

Before I made my big decision, I Googled Minnesota, Minneapolis, the route from Thunder Bay to Sault Ste. Marie through Minnesota, Wisconsin, and Michigan, and the Minnesota Zen Center.

There was a Zen poetry presentation at the Zen Center that night, with an admission price of ninety bucks per person.

Minnesota was described as a state with a lot of lakes and numerous tourist attractions that featured Paul Bunyan, not to mention Babe, the Blue Ox, and Minneapolis was described as the fittest city in America, the home of many Fortune 500 companies, and as the place where the Mississippi River started.

You could step across the Mississippi in Mineapolis, or walk across it, using a pathway made of stepping stones, close to its source, before it turned into the big, wide, river that bisected America and ran all the way down to the Gulf of Mexico.

Minneapolis was a city of over three million people and the home to the Minnesota Vikings of the NFL as well as the Minnesota Wild of the NHL.

The Minnesota Zen Center, in Minneapolis, was made famous by Natalie Goldberg, who wrote about it in a number of her books, after studying there for about fifteen years.

Robert Pirsig, the author of Zen And The Art Of Motorcycle Maintenance, had also studied at the MZC, before his famous book came out.

Goldberg had a new book out,

Natalie Goldberg's first book, Writing Down

the Bones: Freeing the Writer Within (Shambhala), was a surprise hit when it was published. The first print run was ten thousand copies but it sold more than a million copies in ten languages.

She spent twelve years studying with Zen teacher Katagiri Roshi in Minnesota. She began writing and painting soon after beginning her Zen studies.

Wild Mind, my favourite book by Natalie Goldberg, was considered the classic writing guide. It follows Zen tradition—connecting the craft of writing with the source of creative power. She gives compassionate, practical, and often humorous advice about how to find time to write, how to discover your personal style, how to make sentences come alive, and how to overcome procrastination and writer's block -- including more than thirty provocative "Try this" exercises to get your pen moving.

Write about what you remember, she suggests. Write about what you forget.

Some of her other well-known writing prompts are: "I am looking at", "I know", I don't know, "I am thinking of", and I am not thinking of.

Her latest book was called The True Secret of Writing, and it was called Goldberg's Zen boot camp for writers.

Shut up and write, she advises.

But, of course, Goldberg would not be at the Zen Center, running writing workshops. She was down in New Mexico, leading writing workshops that were described as Zen retreats with writing practice.

And so I decided to skip Minneapolis, Minnesota, as well as Wisconsin and northern Michigan, and stay in Canada for my trip from West to East. I would see Lake Superior instead of the famous Zen Center.

5. Waking Up In Manitoba

The day I started my journey across Canada, I woke up in Cold Lake without an alarm clock at around five thirty and was out the door, in the car, ready to go by seven thirty.

My back, injured the year before, felt very sore. Aside from that, I was feeling good to go. My back gives me some referred pain, so I feel it in my hamstrings, sometimes, or in my butt. I had spent a week moving furniture and cleaning, so the pain had been building.

I made an appointment to see Mecelle, the magic reflexologist, on Monday, before I left, but I canceled it, as I really wanted to get on the road again.

Pulling out of the parking lot, I started to feel real good. My back felt a bit better, I thought. As I drove around the big pot holes on the streets leading to the highway out of town, I wondered if my back issues were all psychosomatic, in my head, not related to nerve or spine problems at all, because -- minute by minute -- I felt better.

Maybe it was just the excitement of starting a

journey, going home, getting on the road again.

As I pulled out of the driveway, I clicked on the car radio and listened to the CBC News.

The floods in Toronto and Calgary were still in the news, along with Canmore and Banff, but the big news was about a train derailment and explosion in Lac Megantic, Quebec. A train carrying crude oil went off the rails, crashed, exploded, wiped out a big part of the town, and freaked out people across the country. The list of people killed and missing, after the crash, kept growing.

Urban flooding was expected to increase with global warming, one report said.

A thunderstorm was heading for eastern Manitoba and the western corner of Northern Ontario, with a possibility of tornadoes.

I wondered if I could time my trip to avoid the big rain storm.

The highway heading out of town, to the south, is better than 55, on the 55th parallel, going to Lac La Biche. As I went up the hill I watched Cold Lake disappear in my rear-view mirror and I checked in with my feelings, in my heart, high heart chakra, and tan tien. It was not sadness I felt. I was elated.

That feeling grew as I drove down the long hill to the cut-off for The Elizabeth Settlement and the cut-off for Lloyd.

The Elizabeth Settlement is a little Metis town that looks a little rough, shall we say. Lloyd is Lloydminister, an oil town on the border between Alberta and Saskatchewan.

I had driven the two-lane highway down to Lloyd before, but it looked and felt better this time than in the past, for some reason. The morning sun was burning off some low lying fog. I noticed hundreds of cobwebs in a little swamp made it look magical. In the bush of the Cold Lake Indian Reserve, I saw cattle wandering around. It is the only place I have seen cattle in the woods, or the forest, instead of an open field.

South of the Settlement and the Reserve, the country opens up, and it looks more like the oil patch, as the black silos of insitu operations appear more and more often and the horizon spreads out so you can see for miles and miles.

The landscape really changes around Frog Lake, the site of a historic battle between aboriginals and whites, long ago, but not forgotten. I felt guilty, driving through the region, but noticed it was looking good. There was oil under the ground and cattle grazed in rolling wheat land, on top of the ground. The landscape and the land both looked rich.

The more I drove through the eastern corner of the southern section of Northern Alberta, the happier I felt. The road rolled out, smooth and straight, with a few hills and curves, the fog patches were replaced by a clear, sunny, day, and I felt happier and happier.

There's an area south of Elizabeth, around the Beaver River, with hills, where the highway curves through the river valley, that reminded me of Muskoka a great deal.

That highway leads out of Alberta to a highway that traces the border with Saskatchewan and there is no sign that says Welcome To Saskatchewan, here, but in my rear-view mirror I saw one that said Welcome To Alberta.

And I said, out lood, Woooooooooohooooooooo!

I was surprised at myself. I felt enormously elated to be on my way, driving into the next province, away from the place I called home for the past two years.

That feeling grew all the way down to Lloydminister, where I stopped for cheap gas. I had been to Lloyd a couple of times in the past, but it had never looked so good, to me.

Maybe it was the time of year. Early July is early summer in this part of the world. And Lloyd looked like it was booming. It looked like a beautiful mid-size city in the mid-west, straddling the meridian that marks the border between Alberta and Saskatchewan.

I knew the place well enough to make the turn onto the Yellowhead Highway without looking for signs, and that was a good thing, as Lloyd was a little shy about roadsigns. The Yellowhead Highway was under construction, in town, so maybe some of the signage was obscured, or missing, or something.

The Saskatchewan side of Lloyd looks richer and greener. You drive by a big Husky oil refinery and as you head east the horizon gets bigger and bigger.

The highway turns into a long, straight stretch with beautiful views of farmland dotted with forest to the distant horizon on both sides and a long way into the distance.

I saw a dead deer, hit by a car, on the side of the highway, between Lloyd and The Battlefords. I saw a few magpies before Lloyd but left behind my new favourite bird as I drove east on the Yellowhead beside the North Saskatchewan River.

I crossed the big, meandering, brown river south of Frog Lake and then again a couple of times in The Battlefords.

North and South Battleford, now called The Battlefords, looked fantastic, with its big bridges rivaling the yellow bridge over the North Saskatchewan just before you leave Alberta for beauty.

The highway from The Battlefords to Saskatoon is not a long and winding road, it is incredibly straight and flat and add to that the fact that there were fewer and fewer cars on the road with me, and my journey changed.

That feeling of elation that started when I left Cold Lake and was amplified when I left Alberta grew until I hit Saskatoon at noon, half an hour ahead of schedule, and I realized I was feeling ecstatic.

I got stuck in traffic, merging with the traffic circle, in Saskatoon, and my phone rang a few times, but I let everybody leave voice messages.

The magic reflexologist phoned to re-book my appointment. Concordia University in Portland, Oregan, wanted me to take their online M.Ed. program, specializing in adolescent literature. My brother wondered when I would be arriving.

The traffic circle that is supposed to make traveling around Saskatoon was under construction and closed roads led me out of town in an area I did not want to be in, as it was not connected to the highway out of town, going south to Regina.

Instead, I saw an area with three places called snow dumps, beside a landfill site, and it looked as though the snow dumps were being used as landfill sites.

One had a small mountain of what looked like

dirty brown sand and litter, but turned out to be unmelted snow from last winter, with a covering of debris.

Saskatoon must get a lot of snow, compared to Cold Lake, to have a mountain left over at the end of June and the start of July.

I lost around an hour, getting turned around, south of Saskatoon, as I had to go north, back into town, and then across town, to find the exit.

That feeling of elation returned as I learned I had found the highway heading south to the capital city of Saskatchewan.

I stopped for gas at a place just outside the south entrance and exit to Saskatoon and it was clear sailing on a long, straight, flat, well-maintained highway, with little traffic, all the way down to Regina.

It felt as though the entire route was on a slight decline, it was all downhill, and I could coast from Saskatoon to Regina, but that was an illusion.

It was so quiet, like the highway from The Battlefords to Saskatoon, that it was easy for me to meditate, as I drove, with nothing to do except count breaths and zone out.

I counted roadkill at the side of the highway, too. There were three big coyotes south of Saskatoon.

Saskatoon looked very good, to me, as I had not been to a city for several months, and the place looked like it was booming. I kept thinking about how much I would love to live there as the Writer In Residence, as they have a famous program at their library.

When I lived in Ontario, I thought of the residencey in Saskatoon as a far-off, exotic, adventure in a town that was way up north. After a couple of years in Cold Lake, Saskatoon looked like a sparkling city in the sunny south, an oasis of urban civilization, with busy streets, crowded city blocks, hundreds of people out for walks, and lots of big buildings.

The other thing I noticed in Saskatoon were the trees. There was a greater variety of trees. Around Cold Lake and all through northern Alberta, there is a forest of aspen and black spruce, with very little variety. Saskatoon had lots of variety, and that made me feel very happy. I burst into a big smile I had not used for months.

I thought I saw Joni Mitchell, several times.

In my head, I composed a song about Diefenbaker Drive and it included a line about seeing Joni Mitchell twenty-seven times.

I thought about getting a Saskatchewan Roughriders jersey for a running back with the number 2 and the name Saskatoon as the BTO song about running back to Saskatoon played in the radio in my head.

Regina was a bustling city, too, but easier to get through, as they had some signage indicating the intersection with the Trans-Canada Highway, heading west to Calgary, Canmore, Banff, and Vancouver, and east, to where I wanted to go.

There was a sign that said This Way To Winnipeg. It was Highway 1A, with a maple leaf behind the number and the letter, and it made me smile.

I saw red-wing blackbirds and no more magpies and felt ecstatic, even when I saw a few racoons and a porcupine on the side of the highway.

The four lane highway from Lloyd to Battleford was long, flat, straight, and quiet, and the stretch from Battleford to Saskatoon was the same only moreso, while the highway south from Sasktatoon to Regina was more of the same time ten, but the Trans-Canada Highway, four lanes separated by a median so wide you lost sight of the highway going west, was so long, straight, flat, and quiet, it inspired me to change the name of this book from The Long Quiet Canadian Highway to The Never-Ending Peaceful Canadian Highway.

The TCH in my mirror and ahed of me was flat and straight to both horizons and the view out my windows, left and right, was the same, but across fields of grain, as I drove past the places where two of my mentors came from: Weyburn and Estevan.

I met W.O. Mitchell and Eli Mandel in the mountains, in the Rocky Mountains of Banff, but this was where they came from, the place they wrote about the best: where the horizon is so distant that roads, train tracks, and highways reach the vanishing point.

I reached the vanishing point again and again and saw that it was an illusion as the highway went on and on and on.

Perfect for driving meditation.

I had lots of thoughts but spent most of my time empty-minded, until my brother phoned.

One of the most impressive sights I saw in Saskatchewan, aside from the fantastic fields of wheat stretching to the horizon in every direction, was a big field of wind turbines, enormous fans, not far from where W.O. Mitchell wrote Who Has Seen The Wind, turning air into energy, instead of coal, crude oil, or tar sands.

Why were so many people opposed to wind energy? Nobody wanted a wind farm in their back yard or close to where they lived, apparently, but I thought they looked beautiful, impressive, magnificent.

And they didn't pollute the sky with coal smoke, and they didn't pollute the rivers with oil, or use a lot of water, or need contaminated tailing ponds, or huge holes in the ground, or pipelines criss-crossing the continent that broke and caused oil spills, or railway cars full of crude that ran off the rails and exploded, blowing up towns like Lac Megantic.

I made it to Brandon, and could have gone on to Winnipeg, but I thought I would call it a day at my destination for the first section of my journey. I had driven from Alberta across Saskatchewan to Manitoba. I fell asleep dreaming about wheat, thinking about the Wheat Belly Diet, seeing fields of wheat in my dreams, and then nothing.

I had a scary thought: Day One of my trip was so great, with ideal weather, a beautiful landscape with one fantastic-looking scene after another, like a nature film with high production values, all those golden nugget yellow fields stretching to the far distant horizons .... How could Day 2 be any better?

What horror awaited me in Manitoba?

The traffic circle that is supposed to take cars and trucks around Winnipeg was a nightmare, when I passed through on my way out west two years earlier.

My first job as a teacher, with Frontier

College, while I was still an undergrad, took me to the prisons of Manitoba. The federal institution, Stony Mountain, the maximum security place, outside of Winnipeg, where a guy from my school was stabbed with a shiv, and died, while I was there. Headingly, the medium security prison in Winnipeg, where the last person to be hanged in Canada was put to death, and the guards showed me the gallows were still in place, and explained why they wanted to use it again. They said the sounds of the executions, at midnight, when the rest of prison population was quiet, so they could hear the last screams of the dying men, or maybe hear their necks snap, had a good effect on the prison, as the other guys were quiet for days afterward.

The prison I spent most of my time at, as a labourer/teacher, for Frontier College, was a minimum security prison in the Whiteshell Provincial Park, a bush camp, with a warden named Web Walls.

Seriously.

Bannock Point Rehabilitation Camp, in the bush beyond Seven Sisters Falls, in the Whiteshell, had died, fallen into ruin, left abandoned, and was likely haunted.

Would I see the ghosts of those terrible prisons when I went to Manitoba?

I had a nightmare about getting in a car crash with a big rig on the traffic circle and winding up in Headingly, the prison where they wanted to hang people, again.

Winnipeg traffic proved to be no problem. Heading east on the Trans-Canada Highway, the traffic circle whisks you by the south end of the city so you don't get slowed down by city traffic for one second or see anything of Winnipeg except a sign for Headingly.

CBC Winnipeg said there was a problem with swimmers' itch at Winnipeg Beach, north of the city.

The endless fields of wheat finally come to an end east of Winnipeg where the first granite boulder can be seen. When I saw that boulder, believe it or not, and I cannot believe it, I yelled.

Granite boulder!

I never thought I would miss granite boulders

or get excited about seeing granite boulders again.

There were more and more granite boulders and then there were granite bedrock outcroppings as the prairie ended and the Canadian Shield began.

The next landmark was Whiteshell Provincial Park.

I lived and worked in Whiteshell Provincial Park one winter, teaching basic literacy skills in Bannock Point Rehab Camp, and I always wondered why there was a park there, as The Whiteshell looked, to me, like so much of Ontario.

While I was in Cold Lake, I met someone who explained it to me. She said that if you live on the prairie and see nothing but prairie all the time, it is thrilling to travel to the edge of the Canadian Shield, at Whiteshell Provincial Park, and see hills, rocks, trees, a mixed forest, instead of flat land and wheat fields spreading out in every direction to the distant horizons.

Once you hit the Whiteshell, it isn't long until you hit Ontario.

Once you hit Ontario, the landscape changes dramatically. There is one rock cut after another after another. It looks like Norway, with all the rock cuts like tunnels leading across the north-west corner of Northern Ontario from the Manitoba border to the town of Nipigon.

There aren't many gas stations on the Trans-Canada, so I got off the highway that goes coast to coast and went down to Nipigon, a rediculously good looking town, with granite bedrock outcroppings and rock cuts leading down to a big blue lake.

The radio station is called the Lake. It was broadcasting storm warning for the area from Nipigon to Thunder Bay, where I was driving, and predicting heavy downpours with the possibility of flooding.

Was Thunder Bay going to be the next Toronto, after Calgary, Canmore, and Banff, with a big flood, just when I was driving into town?

Between Nipigon and Thunder Bay, there were a few bridges under construction, or being reconstructed, with the traffic stopped by lights or somebody waving a stop sign, and I had a close call at one of them.

Several years ago, I got rear-ended while stopped for highway construction in Ontario. My car was totaled but I walked away without a scratch and everybody said, You're lucky to be alive.

Ever since then, I have been hyper alert whenever I've had to stop on a highway, for a light or a sign person, and I've kept my eyes on my rear view mirror, so I can see who's coming and if they're stopping.

When I got hit, the truck behind me did not see the oversized stop sign that a construction worker was waving, furiously, and he said he did not see my little car, either. So, he hit me at full speed and sent my car flying.

Maybe that hit from behind was the whack that put my back out of alignment, all those years ago, and led to my back issues of the past year.

I watched as a truck zoomed up behind me, on the highway between Nipigon and Thunder Bay, where there was jut one lane for traffic over the bridge men were working on. At first it looked as though he was moving too fast to stop in time to avoid hitting me. So, I moved my car so I could get away.

Fortunately, the driver of the big rig did see the stop sign, or the stop lights, and he was able to stop his truck in time, this time.

The skies turned grey, then dark grey, then black, and there were more rock cuts, and for a long time I was driving through dark rock cuts with a dark sky overhead and I felt like Luke Skywalker flying into the the Death Star, in Star Wars.

That image made me laugh, which lightened the mood, but then it started to rain, but I saw something else that made me happy: a big Muskoka Transport truck rolled past me.

I had not seen the word 'Muskoka' on anything since I left Ontario and even the sight of a Muskoka Transport truck was enough to make me smile as I thought about home and the fact that I must be getting closer to home if there was a Muskoka Transport eighteen wheeler hauling something down the hallway.

Going the speed limit, 90 kmh, felt like slow motion, after zipping across Saskatchewan and Manitoba, where the posted limit was 110 and everybody drove at least 10 kmh over.

First it felt like slow motion and then, with a heavy downpour of rain, it felt as though I was driving underwater.

To relieve the gloom, I started singing along with the one album I brought along for the trip: Once In A Blue Moon, by my old buddy, Glen Hornblast.

I already knew all the words to all the songs on the album, and had fun singing them in the rain as I rolled into Thunder Bay: True Blue Forever, Once In A Blue Moon, Loretta, Mary, Evangeline, River, Freedom Train, Isla Mujeres, Le Pont des Arts, Miracle, Homeless, and Tomorrow is a Friend of Mine.

I drove around downtown Thunder Bay for over an hour, looking for a place to stay, and getting to know the city, a bit, wishing it would stop raining so I could see the impressive islands in the bay. Forested cliffs rose up steeply on big islands just off the shore. Huge, old, grain elevators lined the shore.

Rough roads reminded me of Cold Lake.

Lake Superior reminded me of Cold Lake.

I finally found the hotel I was looking for and I hit the sack, but I was too jazzed to sleep, right away. I was sleepless in Thunder Bay.

6. Waking Up In Ontario

When I woke up in Thunder Bay, I knew what I wanted to do. I had debated driving south through Minnesota, to Minneapolis, to the Minnesota Zen Center, and then under Lake Superior, across Wisconsin, and the top of Michigan, to Sault Ste. Marie, as opposed to driving across Northern Ontario, on top of Lake Superior. When I woke up, there was no longer any question about what I wanted to do: Highway 17 from Thunder Bay to Wawa and The Soo.

Driving across Saskatchewan is so incredible, and driving across the prairies is fantastic, while the winding way from the Whiteshell to Nipigon is surprisingly scenic and fascinating, but the North of Superior route is absolutely amazing.

The North Shore of Superior should be on your bucket list. The National Post said that one of the "100 things to do in Canada before you die" was to ride a motorcycle across the North Shore of Lake Superior.

Highway 17 from Sault Ste. Marie to to Thunder Bay in Ontario, Canada has long been known as one of Canada's greatest rides. The twists and turns and ups and downs as this section of the Trans-Canada Highway reveals the shores of Lake Superior make for a holy grail of motorcycle touring.

There is great riding and great views for car drivers, too. The carved rock face, the wild windswept forests, and the lake, so large it's described as an inland sea, make the route one of the best kept secrets in the world.

The Sea To Sky Highway north of Vancouver is stunning and the Earth To Heaven Highway along the coast of Georgian Bay through Muskoka and Parry Sound is awe-inspiring, but the North Shore of Lake Superior makes all the rest look inferior.

This route can be approached from either Sault Ste. Marie or Thunder Bay, of course, but it's best to start in Thunder Bay and go from west to east.

It's a very good idea to do the detour to see the Sleeping Giant, south of Highway 17, just out of Thunder Bay, down to the tip of Sleeping Giant Provincial Park.

The Park is named after a huge island rock

formation that looks like an enormous man made of stone, lying down, with his arms crossed, which is best viewed from Thunder Bay.

Driving around Lake Superior, I said, "Wow!" and "Omigod!" out loud several times.

There are countless incredible views of the big lake with big islands from small mountains and it feels as though it never ends.

There's eight hours of that!

If you stop at every look-out, the trip will take a lot longer than that.

It is better than the Icefields Parkway, between Jasper and Banff. It's longer and ... What do you want to look at: ice-capped mountains, or a huge blue lake with enormous islands, as you travel through mini-mountains?

It is inspiring as well as awe-inspiring and unbelievably beautiful.

It is difficult to meditate while driving this route, but there are thousands of place that look as though they would be great to sit and contemplate the vastness of the lake and the beauty of the landscape.

The highway from The Soo to Sudbury is as straight as the Trans-Canada across the prairie, for long stretches, and so is the highway from Sudbury to Muskoka, in many places.

My goal was to make it from Thunder Bay to Wawa, but in Wawa I knew I would be able to make it to The Soo, and in The Soo I thought I would make it to Sudbury but when I got to Sudbury, I thought I might make it to North Bay and, of course, getting so close to Muskoka made me want to keep on going even though it meant driving in the dark.

The only problem was that I could not see the landscape I loved so much.

However, I was reminded that Muskoka smells great.

At night, lit up, Muskoka looked richer than when I left. It looked as though the district had been spruced up for the start of summer. There were flowers everywhere. Flowers were planted and grew everywhere.

I heard a songbird.

The mixed forest turned into a deciduous

forest, for a long stretch, and then turned into a mixed forest of tall trees, again.

I was home.

It was hard to believe that Sudbury had a population of only 150,000, as it looked a little bigger, and it was even harder to believe that Thunder Bay's population was only 100,000.

A sign said Huntsville was close to 20,000, and that was hard to believe, too, but for the opposite reason.

In the winter, the population of Huntsville goes down a little bit, and in the summer it goes way, way up, of course.

When I got into the hotel across the street from Avery Beach, I plugged in my computer and I got a note from someone I met at the Zen Forest. She said, You sound much happier now and your plans reflect God (good, orderly, direction).

Also, I noticed a posting on Facebook, from the Spirituality Network, that said, "The Universe is saying, Allow me to flow through you unrestricted and you will see the greatest magic you have ever seen." It was a quote from Klaus Joehle.

I thought that described the route from Cold Lake to Muskoka just perfectly.

7. Waking Up In Muskoka

My first morning in Muskoka, I got up early, ish, around seven, showered quick, and headed out the door. Although my expectations were huge, I was not disappointed. Muskoka looked magnificent.

One of the first things I noticed, aside from the blue sky and the deciduous forest surrounding me, was that orange tiger lillies bloomed everywhere, in cultivated and wild gardens, alongside planted flowers and wildflowers.

The air smelled fresh and clean, with no hint of oil or of forest burning. There were no fighter jets flying by in the sky. But what would the lake be like? Could it possibly be as blue, clear, cool, warm, refreshing, and healing as I remembered or imagined it?

Avery Beach, a couple of blocks away, was my first stop. It's a little beach on Hunter's Bay, beside the Trans-Canada Hiking Trail, with a grassy area groomed for sunbathers, a shelter for picnicers, and a picnic table under an enormous white pine tree, for me.

I walked right into the water. It was heaven.

If there is water in heaven, it has to be like this.

The bay looked blue, in the near and far distance, but clear as air when you looked straight down. It felt cool for the first minute I waded in but by the time I got up to my knees it felt as warm as a summer breeze.

Unbelieveably, there was nobody in the water except a little boy, playing with a mini surf board. He said, "Hi!" and his mother immediately yelled at him not to bug me.

I laughed and told her it was alright, so he threw his little surfboard to me and I threw it back like a frisbee, making it go high in the sky but land close to him in the water.

As I walked out, I asked his mom, or his sister, who was sunbathing in a bikini, if she was a Huntsville person and if she knew where I could find the alternative healer I was looking for.

Yes, she said. I'm good friends with her son, but I haven't seen them for a while. I think she is working out of her house, now.

One of the things about small towns that you have to love is that everybody knows everybody and what they are doing and where they are doing it.

The first person I looked for in Muskoka was an alternative healer named Laura Heming.

After looking for her where her business used to be, I asked about her at The Sistas Wellness Kitchen, The Great Vine, and a new naturopath's place. After that, I posed a note on Facebook and looked her up on the internet.

My second stop was at the place where the alternative healer worked the last time I saw her. She worked alongside a Registered Massage Therapist in a house about a block away from the main street of town, which was called Main Street, close to the centre of town, at the intersection of Main and Centre Street.

But there was no sign of her there.

My third stop was for breakfast at Soul Sistas Wellness Kitchen, in their new kitchen. When I lived in Muskoka several years ago, I did a story about Soul Sistas moving from the area at the back of a health food place called The Great Vine to a new location across the alley in the next building. I did a follow-up story when they moved from there to a cool location by the lights and the bridge over the river in the heart of town. They made that space look great, using lots of wood inside, and with a very artsy table outside that looked like it was carved out of granite. It was the home of the little writers group in Huntsville and I joined them there a few times when I was in the area.

Soul Sistas had a new location a few blocks away in a new building which gave them a lot more room for their kitchen and seating as well as a patio area outside.

Lorraine Morin, the owner of Soul Sistas, remembered me, which I thought was nice, since I'd been away for years, and we had a little chat.

Soul Sistas Wellness Kitchen features organic, vegan, vegetarian, gluten-free, and dairy-free dishes, and makes them all very yummy. They have fresh wholesome foods, specialty coffees and teas, fresh juices, smoothies, salads, wraps, soups, and so on. Everything was homemade with local, fresh, healthy ingredients.

The restaurant in heaven, I caught myself

thinking, will have to be just like this.

But then I realized that I didn't have to compare everything in Muskoka to things in heaven, or vice versa, because I was in heaven!

Everybody in Soul Sistas knew the alternative healer I was looking for but nobody knew where she was, for sure. They said there was a naturopath and a group of alternative healers on the road leading out of town, to the south, and they thought maybe the alternative healer I was looking for had moved there.

I checked out both locations and met friendly people in good-looking venues but they had no information about the alternative healer I was looking for.

Catherine Cole at The Great Vine took a few seconds to look up her phone number and write it down for me. The Great Vine is a passionate, eclectic, one-stop, shop that offers a dynamic range of products in the area of complementary health.

I phoned Laura, finally, left a message, sent her another message on Facebook, and then got in touch with her the old fashioned way: I went to her house.

Freedom Place, her business, was now located on the second floor of her house. And the house looked great. It had a new roof, a fresh coat of paint, newly cut grass, and good looking gardens. It was a two and a half story wood frame white house with blue treem. I remembered when she bought it, from a mutual friend, and there was a problem with plumbing or water in the area. There was a boarder living upstairs.

It looked like it had all been fixed.

Looks great! I said.

It's coming, she said. It's coming.

She asked me if I wanted to go for teach but I told her what I really wanted was to make an appointment.

Tomorrow at 3, she said.

We hugged. It was a long, healing hug.

She looked happy, but after that hug I felt sad, for some reason. And that sadness stayed with me for an hour.

To cheer myself up, I thought I'd go get a slice of Pizza Pizza, something they don't have out west, in

Alberta, or anywhere except Ontario.

My brother phoned while I was driving around the little hill town with the river running through it. He said he was getting ready to go a re-enactement as he was leaving the next day to drive to Upper Canada Village.

He asked me where I kept my laptop at night, while traveling, and told me not to leave it in my car.

Don't trust anyone! he said.

I told him I kept my laptop with me so I could write late into the night, but I trusted everyone.

My brother asked where I was staying and when I told him I was in a hotel for a few days and then going camping, he said, Good, you deserve a break today, afte the year you've had.

Yeah, I said. I guess.

The doc said I was going to die, I had GBS, I'd never walk or work again. But I proved him wrong.

So what if I looked out of shape and overweight. I was alive! I felt great!

I was happy just to be alive, and to be able to walk, so everything else was a bonus. And there was so much more. I was in Muskoka, again, and the marathon was about to begin.

Once again, I found myself in heaven, surrounded by devas, and I had to remember to work on enlightenment.

Pizza Pizza was right beside Algonquin Outfitters. I dropped in to ask about renting a canoe. First I talked to a woman who told me all about the flood that hit the store and the town in the springtime.

She showed me how high up the water and mud had been in the store, and how strange it was for them to be able to paddle out the door and over to the restaurant on the hill on the other side of the river.

You have an awesome attitude, I said, and I told her I was from Alberta so I knew a bit about the flood that hit Canmore, Banff, and Calgary, that summer.

She told me about the flood that hit Toronto a few days earlier.

Weird, wild, weather, we both said at the same time. Global warming.

To rent a canoe, I had to phone their Algonquin Park store. They had two rental locations and needed just one reservation person, a high school kid working there told me. I know it sounds crazy, he said, but it got confusing.

As I walked around town, down the steps by the Pub On The Dock, across the dock to the parking lot behind Algonquin Outfitters, feeling the warm sun and the cool breeze, looking at the blue water, I thought about living in this beautiful warm place. it's different in the winter, I knew.

When I went by the high school, I could not help but notice the big new granite fieldstone building called Summit Place, built for the G8, but not used for that.

It upstaged the high school, which used to dominate this area beside the meandering river.

I went to the beach for the afternoon. From Avery Beach, Huntsville looks like a forested hill. It's almost completely hidden, behind green, leafy, deciduous trees.

I felt sad, sitting there, for a moment. What

happened to the ecstasy and inspiration I felt in Northern Ontario, looking at the amazing views of Lake Superior?

For a moment I felt like a guy with an inferiority complex. What was going on?

But then I remembered what was going on in the near future. The marathon would be great. And a week after the marathon there was a reunion planned for my old hometown. Two hundred and fifty tickets had been sold. The two most beautiful women from that time and place had both asked me to be their dates for the reunion. And one of them wanted to go camping and canoeing with me after the reunion.

I remembered I was in heaven with devas but I still had to work on enlightenment.

In the afternoon, I returned to Avery Beach, to write in the sun, and swim, and celebrate heavenly summer in Muskoka.

I took a trip up to Arrowhead Park, to check on reservations for later in the month, when I planned to return to Muskoka for a camping date.

My first kiss girlfriend from back in the day, as

they say, wanted to go camping.

At six o'clock a group of novel marathoners was planning, via Facebook, to get together at the Pub On The Docks, downtown, so I joined them.

Some veteran MNMers from out of town arrive a day early, instead of arriving just in time, like the newbies, and have a reunion.

When I found a group of seven writerly artists sitting outside at two tables with beers in front of them, they greeted me with applause, so I smiled and nodded and went around the table to hug the people I knew and get introduced to the others. There were a few I knew from facebook as novel marathoners who joined the MNM while I was away.

Dawn Huddleston, a marathon producer, looking after social media, gave me the best greeting, saying, "It's so good to see you alive, walking, looking healthy, and to have you here for the marathon."

Thanks, I said. Y'es, it's good to be alive and well and in Muskoka for a marathon.

After ordering a Guiness, I was unusually

talkative.My beer order raised eyebrows as everybody knows I'm a non-drinker.

Guiness is good for you, I aid, raising my glass, repeating theor old slogan, and a few people said, I shoulve have ordered a Guiness, or I love Guiness.

I asked the people sitting around me questions about the marathon and their writing and told a few stories about old Lake, Alberta, and some of the legends of the MNM.

I told the stroy about starting the MNM with Mel Malton,how I moved to Muskoka after starting a Novel Marathon in Owen Sound, when I lived there, and how I tried to get one going in Gravenhurst for a few years, and how Melt gut us hooked up in a bout half an hour in Huntsville after I told her about the marathon in O.S.

Let's do it, she said.

She called Kareen Burns, a friend, who made us official members of the Huntsville Festival of the Arts, and made a cold call to the Muskoka Literacy Council, to see if they would like to be the recipient of funds raised from the special event we were planning as a part of the Festival of the Arts.

Okay they said.

Mel and Kareen found us a great location in an old store on Main Street, that was empty, and we were off.

I drank about an inch of Guinness as we talked into the night and wound up closing the joint with two wild women from Owen Sound who had done A Novel Marathon and the Muskoka Novel Marathon.

I was in heaven with devas and, despite a little Guinness, remembered I still had to work on enlightenment.

At some point in the evening, they asked me about Cold Lake, and I said I liked it, even though I was a bit of a fish out of cold water, in a Catholic school on the oil patch, between a military air force base and an air weapons range, with fighter jets in the sky all the time, but my high school side of the K to 12 school was closing, due to declining enrollment, and other issues, so I was free again.

You should be here, Karen Wehrstein said. Move to Muskoka where everybody loves you.

Karen was a witch, she told me, years ago.

You should listen to God, she said. Open up your heart and get the message.

She talks like that sometimes.

So I told her the story about my awakening, briefly, how I tried to open up and get the message from the great beyond, and how I woke up one summer after several years at the Zen Forest, and again at a long weekend workshop with my New Age guru.

You know that feeling you get with a peak experience? I said. When you feel connected to everything, at one with the universe .... All that?

Well, I went on and on, I stayed in that zone for months and did a tour of yoga studios, et cetera, across Central Ontario, teaching Zen Forest style meditation, with Reiki self massage, and qigong energy exercises, plus some past life work and future healing.

Then what? Karen said.

Well, I wasn't in the Zen zone, any more, so I looked for a teaching gig, got hired to teach CanLit in China, but took a job in Canada, at the last second, instead.

Cold Lake, she said.

Like Sully, in Avatar, I said.

You even lost your legs, Dawn said, like the guy in Avatar.

I had never made that connection before.

The two women who had been to both the Owen Sound novel marathon, called A Novel Marathon, and the Muskoka Novel Marathon, and I closed the Pub On The Docks, that night. They talked me into staying for the entire marathon, instead of just writing with the gang for one night. They said Saturday night, with Nuit Blanche happening on the street in front of the marathon location, was great, they said. The food was great, the people were great, and the cause was great. Novel marathoners joined in the action on the street at night, late, and I could join them.

That clinched it for me.

We had a good night. Would be able to wake up for the novel marathon the next day?

Waking Up At The Muskoka Novel Marathon

The 12 annual Muskoka Novel Marathon was the biggest. But would it be the best?

It started well, if a little slowly, with a lot of introductions, a reading of the rules and regs, and so on.

I spent the afternoon helping out with the set-up, filling the loot bags the marathoners got when they arrived, looking for string in the stores downtown, and across the river, and then disappearing so I could make my 3:00 p.m. appointment with Laura.

And then I went back to the marathon.

The appointment with Laura was just like in the old days, when I used to see her, so she could fix my sore foot. I had plantar fascietous for a few years. We had some great conversations about spirituality, back in the day, and we picked up right where we left off, more or less. She was much more in the zone and I was more out of it.

First I told her my story about waking up in the Zen Forest and with a New Age guru, going on tour as a Zen meditation teacher and qigong healer, followed by a desire to return to working as a teacher full-time, going to Alberta, instead of China, living in the oil patch between the military air force base and the air weapons testing range, getting exhausted the first year, going back for the second year, getting a stabbing pain in the back, going to a chiropractor, having the pain go away, losing my legs, going to the neurology emergency specialist, the safety pin story, and then healing with the help of a gifted alternative healer who called herself a reflexologist, and a physiotherapist who did acupuncture, plus a lot of time in the gym and the pool.

Well, what will we do for you today? she asked.

I dunno, I said. My feet feel swollen and I've had some back pain since I got to town and helped out with the marathon set-up.

You drove across Canada? she said. Sitting in the car for three days can be hard on the back, she added. Sitting like that can cut off circulation to the legs and lead to back pain and an ache in the butt and hamstrings.

She said, You could be out of alignment because you were supposed to go to China, to study Chinese medicine, but you went out west, to Alberta, instead.

Instead of working on my feet the way she used to, she told me to take off most of my clothes and get on her healing table with a blanket pulled over me.

She worked on my feet, first, doing reflexology, and then massaged my back, using hot rocks and a pain-reducing spray.

The hot rocks did not feel like rocks, at all; it felt as though she was using nothing but massage lotion. The spray felt very hot, so I asked her what it was, and she told me most people experience it as cool, instead of hot.

I asked her what she was doing, and she said she was working on draining my lymphatic system, as I had a lot of poison in my body, and she had a new technique that would help with neck and back pain.

She went to a workshop to pick up the trick, or technique, she said. And she had been to Mexico, after a trip to Peru, to work with native elders, learning more and more about healing.

She also told me she had reading a series of books by Anastasia.

Who? I said.

Where have you been? she said.

Alberta, I said.

Several years ago, information came out of Russia about an amazing being named Anastasia, who lived in the Siberian forests, called the Taiga. She possessed unique powers.

The information was published in a book called Anastasia, with a portrait of a beautiful blonde on the cover, with the caption: "I exist for those for whom I exist."

This book divided the people who read it into those who believe it and those who don't believe.

The story is all about a young woman named Anastasia who lives in the Taiga, absolutely alone, practically without clothes or any stored food.

She is a descendant of the people who lived there for millennia and who had a very different civilization from ours.

Anastasia was born near her grandfather and

great-grandfather, who were still alive and who pass on to her the wisdom of previous generations.

She exists in complete harmony with nature. Trees, animals, and birds surround and protect her.

Her most devoted friends are a she-wolf, a mother bear, and a squirrel. They bring cedar nuts straight to the palm of her hand.

Beetles and other small insects give her the information about her environment.

She knows everything about the urgent problems of our ailing society, and is ready to help us.

Her mission is centered on helping people to pass through "the period of Dark Forces."

The information about Anastasia came through a Siberian businessman named Vladimir Megre. Anastasia fell in love with him and realized he was the person who could get her message to others.

Megre spent a lot of time with her, not knowing if he believed her or not.

She told him about her life, her vision of God and Man, about her dreams and thoughts.   He saw how wild animals obeyed her. He saw her demonstrate telepathic ability that enabled her to connect with any human being at any distance, and to see any problem or situation in other countries.

Anastasia told Megre he was to write a series of books about her, and she committed him to write absolutely frankly about everything that he had learned from her or experienced with her — even about their intimate relations.

Megre did what she told him to. He described everything he had learned and experienced.

There are seven books in the series about Anastasia, called Ringing Cedars of Russia.

The books about Anastasia have created a spiritual awakeing in Russia. Millions of people respond to the books from their hearts. People write lots of letters, paint pictures, compose verses, and write songs dedicated to Anastasia and Megre.

Centers and clubs named "Anastasia" have been created in different parts of Russia, and an Anastasia Coordination Center has been established in Moscow.

The books about Anastasia are "best sellers" in Russia. Other people have written books about Anastasia, claiming that they are getting information from her.

The first thing she addresses is the ecological problem facing the planet. She says it cannot be solved without restoring our lost bond with Nature and Mother Earth.

Laura Heming told me a bit about her trips to Peru and Mexico, the work she did there, how "at home" she felt in the places where she worked with elders, there, and how it had changed the way she works.

I don't advertise, any more, she said, and I now have what I call a divine secretary, or receptionist. I manifest my clients, she said. I just put it out there, how many clients I would like, and when I would like them, and then the phone rings, so I can book them in.

I wanted one more client for this afternoon, she added, and you called, so here we are.

She walked me out and showed me her new garden and her apple tree.

An apple tree in northern Muskoka? I said. You're growing things the way they do in Findhorn!

As I was leaving, I told her that I really liked hearing her stories and I thought that a lot of people would just love to hear them. Thousand and thousands.

Maybe that will be my new job, I told her.

After telling her what the New Age guru said about June, July, and the autumn, with portals open, time to rest and re-group, and then a period with new energy and opportunities, when what was impossible and unimaginable would become probable, she said that resonated with the things she had been studying. And she agreed that maybe that would be my new job: telling the world about healers like her.

I was asked to lead the marathoners in a little qigong exercise that was good for writers, Dawn and Karen went over the info in the handbook they prepared for everybody in the MNM, and then there was a little countdown leading to the time everybody could begin writing, and we were off!

A library-like silence descended on the novel marathon space. All that could be heard for a long was the clicking of keys as writers worked their computer keyboards and it sounded like insects working away in a forest.

I wrote until two in the morning, the first night, and several marathoners were still working away when I left.

Everybody got together for breakfast, at the marathon location, and lunch, and dinner, and a lot of words were written, while lots of visitors wandered through the long rows of tables where the writers were pounding out their novel stories.

Saturday, the second day of the marathon, was Nuit Blanche North, which was billed as a bold, interactive, multi-arts, street festival. Nuit Blanche brought a lot of people to town to see different events happening on the street in front of the marathon location and on the river by the bridge downtown. There was a poetry jam, a sound installation they said was for receiving and transmitting messages through the earth energy grid, a cardboard village where kids could create their own houses, a variety show, buskers, jugglers, acrobats, stilt walkers, art installations, a story-telling troll, a tie making place, big scarecrows on floating docks by the bridge downtown, sculptures of nomads made of wound branches, an enchanted forest made out of recycled newspaper, story telling, an art installation displaying living off the grid in a tiny makeshift house made of wooden skids, a mini-opera on the town docks, and more, including Buzz, a 20 foot inflatable mosquito, attached to the building right across the street from the marathon.

Novel marathoners wrote on the street, after moving desks and computers outside, and wrote haikus for donations to our literacy group.

There was a fire show, a special musical performance with a dozen trombonists positioned along the Muskoka River by the town docks, and a midnight cabaret show.

The cabaret had music, dance, comedy, acrobatics, and drag queens in performance.

After all that entertainment, half the writers were still up for writing, and worked until two or three in the morning.

A couple of writers were still working at four.

I was one of those writers.

I realized that, once again, I was surrounded

by devas, and divas, in heaven, but I had to keep working on enlightenment. And so, I made a date to go to church in the morning.

Trinity United Church, up the street, a bit, had a service at ten in the morning.

Would I be able to wake up in time for that service?

8. Waking Up In Muskoka Again

Write about what you remember, Natalie Goldberg suggests. Write about what you forget.

I remember Cold Lake and Northern Alberta, yelling woo-hoo when I crossed the border into Saskatchewan, the main street of Lloydminister which is the border between Alberta and Saskatchewan, the long quiet highway from Lloyd to The Battlefords, the North Saskatchewan River, the bridges over the river, and Saskatoon. I remember the long, quiet, Canadian highway form Saskatoon to Regina, and from Regina to Brandon, the home of The Wheat Kings, and from Brandon to Winnipeg, and how the highway changed after Winnipeg.

I remember the first granite boulder I saw after crossing the prairies, the landscape of Whiteshell Provincial Park, which looked like Muskoka, the granite bedrock outcroppings and rock cuts around Nipigon, that made it look like Norway, and seeing a Muskoka Transport truck up there, which made me feel at home.

I remember Thunder Bay and Sault Ste. Marie

and the incredible highway connecting them, over the top of Lake Superior, and how superior that route was to the Sea To Sky Highway in B.C., the Icefields Parkway in Alberta, the Earth To Heaven Highway in Ontario, and every other highway I've seen in Canada, the U.S.A., and the rest of the world.

I remember debating the pros and cons of going through the U.S.A. or staying in Canada, going through Minnesota to Minneapolis to see the Minnesota Zen Center, where Natalie Goldberg studied before she wrote Wild Mind and where Robert Pirsig studied before writing Zen And The Art Of Motorcycle Maintenance.

I remember waking up in Thunder Bay and knowing that I wanted to see Lake Superior and the big hills or small mountains on the North of Superior route and I remember saying, out loud, Wow! and Omigod! several times as spectacular views of lake and forest and huge hills with a highway running through them appeared again and again.

I remember the feeling there was a tractor beam pulling me all the way across Canada, from

Cold Lake to Muskoka, and how intense that feeling became when I reached The Soo and Sudbury, inspiring me to keep on driving into the night, until I reached Huntsville, the home of the Muskoka Novel Marathon.

I don't remember meditating, but I know I did. I don't remember driving for hours and hours and miles and miles across half of Canada. I don't remember getting bored on the trip. I don't remember all the great ideas I had, that I was sure I would remember, when I wasn't meditating, on the trip.

I remember recognizing the smell of Muskoka. It was like a freshwater lake and fresh air and a mixed forest of tall trees.

I remember the start of the novel marathon and I remember Nuit Blanche but I don't remember the hours in between when I wrote eighty or ninety pages.

Right now I am looking at the novel marathon room in Club 55 at the Huntsville Town Hall. It is five o'clock in the morning and I am looking at four long rows of tables, littered with laptop computers and the bottles the writers used for whatever they were drinking. There is a chaos of chairs on both sides of the tables, where the writers sat, and there are writers in sleeping bags on the floor under the tables.

I can hear several people snoring.

I am looking at the scoreboard, where the marathoners post their page titles, every time they write another ten. They write their names and totals on multi-coloured strips of paper six inches long and stick them to the shelves of a pine bookcase. There are five rows of those strips of paper in bright colours.

"I am looking at" a Diet Pepsi bottle, a Gatorade bottle, stainless steel water bottles, ceramic mugs, plastic cups, a Tim Horton's coffee cup, a can of Canada Dry gingerale.

I know this novel marathon had a great goal and the writes surpassed that goal. I know they aimed at raising fifteen thousand dollars for literacy and their total was over eighteen thousand, and counting.

I know the writers are exhausted but will rise from their sleeping bags or return from their hotels to write some more, in a few hours, and they will do it again tomorrow, and next year, and for many years to come.

I know that A Novel Marathon and the Muskoka Novel Marathon and even the Great Canadian Winter Novel Marathon, not to mention the Poetry Marathon, were good ideas. They were special event fundraisers that writers loved.

I know that the writers who are attracted to these events are very special people and not many of them are likely to swim across Lake Ontario or even Lake Muskoka, or run across Canada, or Muskoka, but they can write a novel in just three days, and have a great time doing it with a bunch of other writers.

I don't know why this magic formula for a special event fundraiser hasn't swept the nation and the continent and the world, why there aren't novel marathons in every community, coast to coast, and in the U.S.A., the U.K., and Europe, as well as the rest of the planet.

"I am thinking of" coming back next year.

I am not thinking of dedicating my life to starting novel marathons in every region of the country or every community across Canada or anywhere else.

I am not thinking about that school in Cold Lake, where I used to work, or what will happen to the high school half of the building, and where the teachers, EAs, and students will all go next year.

I am not thinking about where I will go next year.

I am thinking of the long, quiet, Canadian highway that connects this country from coast to coast. I remember hitch-hiking back and forth across that highway when I was a kid. I remember the three thousand kilometre trip that took me three days this summer.

I remember my cousin up in Lac La Biche asking me how I was going to drive across half of Canada, if I was going to go through the Northern U.S.A. or stay in Canada, and how could I do it solo, with nobody to talk to, and would I listen to the radio all the time, and not believing me when I said I would meditate while driving.

I barely remember meditating while driving.

I am thinking that it is time to rest and regroup and that this autumn will be a time when new energies and opportunities will present themselves. The impossible and the unimaginable will be possible.

9. Waking Up In The Forest

For my first few nights in Muskoka, I slept in a hotel, across from Avery Beach, swam in Hunter's Bay, and got oriented for the marathon. On the second night of the marathon, I wrote until six in the morning and then slept in a tent in Arrowhead Provincial Park.

On Saturday, I set up the tent, which I have had in my car trunk for a couple of years, never used, and I got a good air mattress to sleep on, in the tent. The two or three person dome tent and the self-inflating mattress both came from Canadian Tire. One is a Coleman, the other is made by Roots.

I love all these things.

I hadn't camped out or slept under the stars, in the forest, or anywhere, in years.

-- Not sure why.

It was fantastic.

After listening to the sleeping novel marathoners snore for a few hours, after the cabaret that ended Nuit Blanche, or was the climax to the night, at two in the morning, after writing an ending for my non-fiction novel called Long Quiet Canadian Highway: Waking Up In Canada, I saw that the sun was up, so I drove up to Arrowhead and crawled into the tent to try sleeping on the air mattress that completely covered the floor of the tent.

I had my doubts about the mattress, because my back has bothered me so much, over the past year, and I wondered about sleeping in the woods, with the night noises of animals, but I faced my little fears and fell fast asleep in the tent in the forested campgrounds in seconds.

Buddha said sleep is a treasure and I had a great treasure, sleeping under the stars and the tall maple trees, in the dome tent, on the Roots air mattress, for a good six hours. I didn't move from the position I took to fall asleep.

At the Zen Forest, we teach sleeping meditation, as well as walking meditation, sitting meditation, and how to meditate all day while doing all your daily activities.

The sleeping position is the one you often see the Buddha in, when shown lying down, in pictures and sculptures, including the new one at the Zen

Forest.

You lie on your right side, with your heart elevated, so it has less work to do, pumping blood all through your body, and you put one hand under your head and the other on your hip.

"That seals in energy," the monk at the Zen Forest says.

It's qigong sleeping.

With your heart working less strenuously and your energy is sealed in, you sleep peacefully and wake up rejuvenated, re-energized, full of energy.

The monk also says we get a lot of energy from the forest. It's not just the fresh air, manufactured by the leaves of the trees, or the sunlight, that filters through the trees, he says.

After writing until six, and sleeping for a few hours, I jumped up and decided to go for a swim.

The beach was not far from my campsite.

There was nobody in the parking lot beside the beach, so I changed into my bathing suit right there, in the great outdoors, hidden from any passersby, changing between the open doors of my car. There were only a few people lying on the beach, in the sun, and a group of little boys with a couple of dads, playing around in the water, despite the fact it was a perfect summer day in Muskoka, ideal for swimming.

I walked right in to the lake, as it was not cold, and I thought about Cold Lake only for a second, as I dove in and swam around.

It had been a long time since I had been in lake water. I had spent lots of time in the swimming pool at CFB Cold Lake, over the winter and the spring, and I had returned to my practice of swimming lengths as soon as the school year ended. But swimming in a lake is quite different than swimming in a pool.

There were no lanes, no bouys, no square shapes or right angles, no music playing, and no swimmers in the lanes beside me, racing with me. There was a sandy beach between the lake and a grassy area, with the green stuff cut short, and the lake had a sandy bottom, for fifty yards or so, and then dropped off.

Arrowhead is classed as a Natural Environment park. It is upstaged completely by the famous Algonquin Provincial Park, not far away. But, like the highway and the drive around the

North Shore of Lake Superior, it is one of the most under-rated places in Canada and, possibly, the world.

Canadians! We do not brag about how great we are or how great our country is.

We brag a bit about hockey and our hockey players. But, for instance, nobody reported on the fact that more than half of the hockey players drafted in the top twenty of the first round of the NHL draft were Canucks. And nobody in Ontario bragged about the fact that more than half of the Canadians drafted in the top twenty of the first round came from the Ontario Hockey League.

All the Wikipedia entry for Arrowhead says is, "Arrowhead Provincial Park is located north of Huntsville, Ontario, Canada, and is part of the Ontario Parks system. A portion of the shoreline of Glacial Lake Algonquin is visible in the park."

There is almost no information about the park online.

There is an enormous amount of information online and in books about Algonquin Park.

Arrowhead is fantastic in all four seasons and it's close to the heart of Muskoka.

I got to know the park in winter, first, as it has fantastic cross-country ski trails. Those trails are used for hiking, in the summer. Some of them are used for inline skating.

It looks beautiful in the winter, covered in snow, with the Christmas trees appearing as the trees in the hardwood forest lose their leaves.

The Big East River meanders through the park and there are a few lakes, not to mention the waterfalls, that are absolutely beautiful.

After swimming across a little lake, and back, in the morning, I did my yoga routine on the beach, very basic, and then soaked up some sun, lying in savasannah, or the corpse position, feeling the opposite of dead. And I had a vision.

I had several visions.

First I had a flashback to the summers of of my childhood, on Gull Lake and Gravenhurst Bay of Lake Muskoka, and the many hours spent in the water, near the water, lying in the sun in savasannah, without knowing anything about the corpse pose or yoga or meditation, except by intuition.

The second vision was like the big picture I

got after waking up in the Zen Forest, at the weekend Oneness workshop with the New Age guru who had gone to India and return as a Blessing Giver. However, instead of seeing a circle of men around the light many people have seen, during near-death experiences, I saw a circle of women.

A couple of years earlier, I had seen Jesus and Buddha, Bodhidharma and Hsui, John of God and the Sai Baba, and on and on. This time I saw Anastasia and some other women.

I saw the "female Jesus", the woman TIME magazine reported on, in a big article with a bold headline that said, Jesus Is Back And She's A Woman.

And I saw Venerable Dhyani Ywahoo, again.

Margot Anand was there.

There were several other woman whose faces I could not see and whose identities I couldn't figure out. Was that Mother Theresa? My mother? My grandmother? Other women I had known and loved? -- Who knows!

Was that Bharanji Namaste? Crystal Dawn? Oriah Mountain Dreamer? Janet Amare?

Lightning Deng is known as the female Jesus, or the second Christ.

The cult that surrounds her is called Eastern Lightning but the official name for the group is the Church of Almighty God. The Protestant group China for Jesus has estimated there are more than a million people in China who are in the group called Eastern Lightning. It is also known as Seven Spirits Sect, Second Saviour Sect, New Power Lord's Church, True Light Sect, and True Way Sect.

They believe God has returned to earth as a woman, born to an ordinary family in the Northern part of China, to guide mankind for the third and last time.

According to the group, the first and second times of active guidance of mankind were as Jehovah of the Old Testament and as Jesus in the New Testament.

It's all explained in a book called Lightning from the Orient. The book says the first coming of Christ was to redeem humanity, while the second is to conquer men's hearts and defeat Satan.

Venerable Dhyani Ywahoo is an extraordinary spiritual teacher of three wisdom paths—the AniYunwiwa (Cherokee), Drikung Kagyu, and Nyingma (Tibetan Buddhist). The Tibetans call her Pema Sangzin Khandro.

She is part of the Vajra Dikini Nunnery, down in the U.S.A., but I met her at the Zen Forest, where she was leading a retreat.

The Buddhist monk and Zen master Thich Thong Tri, who created the Zen Forest, built a special VIP suite for her, attached to the meditation hall in the Zen Forest.

She was leading a group of women called the Vajra Yoginis on a month-long retreat at the Zen Forest while I was working there as a volunteer.

I asked the monk about them, while we were working outside, and they were in the meditation hall, chanting and making mandalas.

The monk shrugged his shoulders and said, Not Zen, but it was clear he held Dhyani Ywahoo in very high regard.

She smiled and nodded when we were introduced and then floated away, as she does.

I would swear on a stack of Bibles, or the Diamond Sutra, or the Kama Sutra, or whatever, that she did not walk, to get from her suite to the meditation hall, she floated a few inches above the ground.

She wore a long gown and it touched the ground, below her feet, and she levitated over the uneven ground of the Zen Forest to travel from one place to another.

Her Facebook page describes her as Venerable Dhyani and says she offers transformational teachings, life coaching, the Peacekeeper curriculum, and Tibetan Buddhist teachings.

She is the author of Voices of Our Ancestors.

She is Chief of the Ani Yun Wiwa (Cherokee) and the Founder of Sunray, an International Organization and NGO dedicated to planetary peace.

Margot Anand is a French author, teacher, seminar leader, and public speaker. She has written numerous books including The Art of Sexual Ecstasy; The Art of Everyday Ecstasy; and The Art of Sexual Magic.

Margot (or "Margo") Anand (Sanskrit "Ananda"=Bliss), studied at the Sorbonne and then Tantra and related disciplines in India. She became notable as one of the first teachers to introduce Tantra and Neotantra to a broad public in Europe and America, and the creator of "SkyDancing Tantra"

Institutes teaching her methods exist in England, France, Switzerland, Germany, The Netherlands, Sweden, Canada and the United States.

Anand is adjunct faculty at Dr. Deepak Chopra's seminars and conferences.

I studied with her at the Omega Holistic Institute, down in New York State, not far from Woodstock, and about an hour north of New York City.

I met her another time I was at Omega for a workshop with Deepak Chopra.

As Shakespeare said, in The Tempest, O, wonder! How many goodly creatures are there here! How beauteous mankind is! O brave new world, That has such people in it!

Or .... Oh, wonder! How many godly creatures there are here! How beauteous people are! O brave new age, that has such women in it!

Once again, I felt as though I was heaven, surrounded by devas, working on enlightenment.

Is this heaven? I said to myself. And I thought I heard a voice saying, No, it's Arrowhead Provincial Park in Muskoka, Ontario, Canada.

The slogan of the MNM this year, written on the back of the official 2013 tee-shirt, is, "I just write what the voices inside my head tell me!"

When I regained consciousness, as Big Bobby Clobber used to say on Air Farce, on CBC Radio and TV, I gave my fuzzy head a shake and wondered if I had been outside and in the sun too long.

I looked around at the lake in Arrowhead Provincial Park.

I remembered that Arrowhead was not named after arrowheads, there were no ancient aboriginal artifacts found in the area, and the arrowhead is a plant that grows in the rivers of the region, which has leaves shaped like arrowheads.

I rejoined the marathoners after breakfast, which was bacon and eggs, something I wanted to miss, before lunch, to write some more, and wrote after lunch, for a while, as well, but found my productivity slowing down as fatigue took over.

It was time to go outside and sleep in the sun, have a siesta, for a little while, but the weather reports said it was over thirty degrees out there.

The night before, after hitting the 20,000 word mark, or 80 pages, I felt as though this book was finished. However, after sleeping in a tent in the park and swimming in the lake in the morning, I realized there were a few things I wanted to add, including the description of the little vision I had while in savassanah beside the lake.

My first big vision, when I woke up in the Zen Forest and at a Oneness workshop a few years earlier, was about a circle of men, all of them famous spiritual leaders and healers. The new vision was about a circle of female spiritual leaders and healers.

I remember when the monk and Zen master told me the Vajra Yoginis were taking over the Zen Forest for a big retreat and he asked me if I could come to work as a volunteer and stay at the ZF while they were there.

I don't think he wanted to be alone with all those women.

They did not need us to do anything for their retreat, other than stay out of their way, and let them use the meditation hall for their workshops.

The monk and I had breakfast before the all-female group got going and then we headed into the forest to work.

We saw them at lunch time, some days, but we didn't talk as they were on a silent retreat, except for when they were chanting in the meditation hall.

During that time, the monk asked me to chop some wood in the wood lot, to turn a pile of dried logs into firewood. After watching me take the axe and split a few logs into fours, he showed me the Zen Forest way.

Oh, I said. Like qigong.

The Zen way, he said.

He demonstrated the Zen way, which co-ordinated breathing in and out with the lifting and falling of the axe, so you could meditate while chopping logs. He said, Your way, you could work all day, maybe two days, but this way, you can chop logs for days without straining muscles.

Focus on the spot where the axe hits the log, he said, and see it going through. That way, the log explodes, and you work effortlessly.

His method worked like magic.

On the last day of the retreat for the vajra yoginis, they were allowed to talk, and the noise they made was fantastic.

They had all sorts of questions for the monk.

One of the women brought her old dog with her, on the retreat, and even though the Zen Forest guidebook said, No pets, the monk appeared happy to see the animal.

The owner of the dog asked the monk if dogs have souls and if they reincarnate.

There is an old joke or Zen parable about a monk being asked that question. In the Zen story, the monk answers with the word "Mu", which sounds like the noise a cat makes but is the

Sanskrit word for nothingness, meaning "it doesn't matter".

But our monk and Zen master said something that surprised me. He said, Yes, and this dog appears to be an old soul, has the look of a being that has been around for many lifetimes.

He also said that many, many people around the world would be thrilled to be reincarnated as that dog, or any cat or dog or other pet in North America, as they are treated so well, fed better than people in Third World Nations, and lived like beings in heaven, compared to many people elsewhere in the world.

Not all the vajra yoginis wanted to yack as soon as they were allowed to, at the end of the retreat. Some of them wandered down to where I was making noise, exploding logs, turning them into firewood, for the winter, using the qigong or Zen Forest method of chopping wood. They just watched without saying anything.

It was shortly after they left and I left that the monk took over the job of exploding logs in the wood lot, making firewood for the wintertime, when he had a heart attack.

He felt severe tightness in his chest and had trouble breathing, he said. And he thought his time was up, he was going to die, as he often told us he would and we would as everything in this life is temporary.

However, we told him about the heart by-pass operation, which was now common, and he wound up having a triple in the hospital in Belleville.

He came out of the anesthetic "just like that", he told me, snapping his fingers, and the doctors were shocked, as well as the guy who put him under.

I woke up fast, he said. One moment I was completely sedated, like being unconscious, and the next moment I was fully awake, without any groggy period of transition.

I had no idea why I remember the story about the monk who survived a heart attack at that moment.

I remember thinking it was odd that the monk had a heart attack, after a lifetime of living in the forest, with lots of fresh air, and working in the forest, getting lots of exercise, and a lifetime of meditating, without smoking, and living a very healthy lifestyle. But then I learned that heart problems are not unusual amongst Asian men.

The monk was convinced he was about to die and gave directions for his funeral service.

No tears! he said. I want only laughter at my funeral.

A woman I met in the Zen Forest, who we called Zenda, looked after the month a lot while he was in the hospital, as she lived nearby, in Belleville. We stayed in touch, through Facebook, in the years after that.

She moved to Vancouver and then I moved to Northern Alberta. And when I told her I was planning to move back to the area around the Zen Forest, she said she wished she could do that, too.

I told her what the New Age guru said about June, July, and September, and how the autumn would be a time when the previously unimaginable would become possible.

10. Waking Up At the MNM

After reaching the 100 page milestone in my marathon novel, I decided to celebrate by going outside and taking a siesta in the hot Muskoka sun somewhere down by the docks on the river in the heart of town.

One of the snorers from the night before had fallen asleep and was snoring loudly under his desk and chair, on the floor, at the novel marathon. The other marathoners were planning to capture the snoring machine on video and post it on Facebook.

What's the old expression? You snooze, you loose.

Why sleep on the floor when you can snooze in heaven?

That's the Zen Forest way!

Believe it or not.

The monk and Zen master liked to tell the story of the King Goose and the Cooked Goose.

It did not sound like any other Zen story I ever heard.

There were two geese, you see, and a farmer looked after them both, feeding them every day and looking out for them. He put down two bowls for them. One bowl had water and the other bowl had a mixture of milk and water. One goose always drank the water but the other goose always went for the milk and water mixture.

I don't get it, I said.

Why would you choose only water when you can have milk and water? the Zen master said. The goose that drank the milk and water was the King Goose, he added. The other one was soon a cooked goose.

What can I say? Zen stories are seldom transparent.

While I was snoozing in the sun, lying in savassanah, again, I had a different sort of vision. It was like my life flashing before my eyes but only with selected scenes from the Muskoka Novel Marathon, more or less in chronological order.

The first MNM was unforgettable. In 2002, we took over an empty jewellry store on the main street and used it as our venue. Shortly after MNM #1, the empty place was taken over by a clothing chain called Plum Loco. The person who named the store joined us for the second MNM, in 2003.

The first year, we had four writers working together in the dusty old store, plus one person working off-site. The second year, we had 14 people in an old restaurant on the main street of Huntsville. Sloan's restaurant, a landmark in Gravenhurst, had a Huntsville location, and when it closed, we moved in.

The third MNM was held in an old bank building that had recently closed and we had an even bigger crowd. We had writers set up on the counter, in the offices, where the tellers worked, and even in the vault. One woman said she wanted to work in the sunless, airless, vault, as it had the atmosphere she needed for inspiration for the novel she was writing.

I think MNM #4 was in Sutherland Hall, a church building beside the Anglican Church, in Huntsville, the year of a major heat wave. The heat was amplified by the architecture or design of Sutherland Hall and we were worried somebody was going to die of heat stroke. Even so, some people still say that was their favourite marathon. The space definitely had a lot of character and atmosphere.

After that, we were tired of leading the MNM, and just wanted to go in the marathon, as writers, so we handed the novel marathon over to the Muskoka Literacy Council, as they were the recipient of the funds raised.

The Muskoka Novel Marathon is an annual event to raise funds and awareness for adult literacy in Muskoka. To date, the event has raised over $80,000.

The first year, we raised over two thousand dollars, with five people. This year, we raised close to twenty thousand, with almost 40 people.

The fund raising results doubled the year the MNM started using social media, especially a website called Canada Helps, that takes online donations for a wide variety of charities.

MNM #5 was held in an old stone school house, not far from downtown Huntsville, and a former marathoner named Sue Kenney made a short documentary about it that is still online, on YouTube and on the MNM website. That was a good but crowded location.

We had a marathoner from Vancouver who

also ran marathons; that is, she was a runner as well as a writer.

MNM #6 and #7 were held in a place called The Learning Centre, not far from the old stone schoolhouse, but quite different in design. We used four big rooms and the lobby so the group was split into separate groups.

The feedback from marathoners was always first rate. The best one I ever got went like this: The MNM is the best event for writers I've been to in my life and also one of the best life events.

Here's a sampler of the other feedback the MNM got:

Writing is a solitary act, but it was great to be in a room with so many writers, especially when they were engrossed in their work. It was like watching writers in their natural habitat.
– Kim Sparks

Honestly, one of the best writer's marathons I've attended. The fellowship was fantastic and it's very much like a family here! Kudos to the organizers!

– Sharon Ledwith

Awesome event! I will be back next year for sure!
– Michael Codato

The MNM is one of my favourite parts of the
writing year. Productivity, inspiration, and
camaraderie—it doesn't get any better than this.
(Also, sleep-deprived writers = funny.)
– Erin Thomas

Best fun I've had in a chair except that one time
when I was 19 with Jerry.
–"me"

This was my second MNM. I thought I knew what
I was in for. This year's experience taught me to
be more open to possibilities and that—at times—a
story has a mind of its own!
- Susan Blakeney

Best memory: Kevin yelling down the hall at the
writers, "COULD YOU BE QUIET? THERE
ARE PEOPLE TRYING TO PROCRASTINATE

HERE!"
–Debra Bennett

This has been a perfect opportunity to experience
novel writing. A kick-ass intro to this art form.
Great organizers and the group is supportive and
FUN!
– Anon

I have enjoyed this experience so much. It helped
me break through a block that I've had for so long.
The supportive humorous loving space gave me
the help I needed. Thank you.
– Laura Heming

Being around writers writing is what I needed.
– Anon

Best memory: Writing my first novel! I did it.
– Anon

Writers have told me the Muskoka Novel
Marathon is one of the best writing experiences in
their lives and one of the best life experiences, too.

-Martin Avery, originator of the Muskoka Novel Marathon and six-time participant

I loved the Novel Marathon experience in 2008! It was a dream come true - I was velcroed to my chair, surrounded by the contagious energy and enthusiasm of so many wonderful and talented people. The words just flowed. If you have always dreamed of writing, but never felt you could spare the time, give yourself this gift and help the Muskoka Literacy Council at the same time. You will love this experience and you will truly become addicted to the Muskoka Novel Marathon!!!
-Evelyn Pollack

MNM 2008 was my first writing marathon. I went in not knowing whether I would be able to produce at a volume that would create a novel and whether that writing would be even vaguely readable. The result: it was an exhausting experience in which I learned that I can indeed produce decent literature in volume and under a tight time constraint: I completed a novelette with enough meat that it will eventually become a complete novel. I also got to meet and talk with fellow writers (during breaks and meals) about sticking points in our writing and about other things in the wider world. It was an enjoyable and worthwhile experience I will happily repeat.

-Herb

Come out and write! It doesn't have to be good; it doesn't have to be winning; it might not even get finished; but, just come out and write with us. If you want to be a writer or if you are a writer, come out and practice with us. There's a manuscript waiting for you to type it at the Muskoka Novel Marathon. Challenge yourself to do something you've always wanted to do: write a novel (in a weekend!). Come to the annual meeting of the weird, the wicked, the wonderful, the sweet, the solemn, the sober, the silly, the sleep-deprived, the stumbling, staring, stuck, un-stuck keyboard punchers at the Muskoka Novel Marathon. A place for you has been reserved.

-five-time participant

I was nervous coming into my first marathon, but

was quickly made welcome by the supportive community of writers I met at the Muskoka Novel Marathon. Besides being able to sit and write an entire novel from beginning to end in just two or three days, I left with a great sense of camaraderie and belonging. Every writer MUST experience the luxury of spending an entire weekend marathon writing! There is nothing else in my writing life that compares to it.
-Kevin Craig

I entered the 2008 MNM at the last minute and with no idea what to expect. What I found was a fun event with a supportive group of writers and volunteers. I'm glad I attended and am looking forward to MNM 2009!
-Dawn Huddlestone

They made me laugh, cry, ponder, belch, wretch, angry, afraid, crazy, love and lose control of my bodily functions - and that was just the authors! Wait till they read you their stories!
-Sharon Ledwith

A fun environment to laugh, learn, and work. The perfect mix of fun and competition, camaderie and rivalry.

-Tracey Lapham

As a first time participant in 2008, I found the MNM experience unleashed a passionate craziness I had forgotten I possessed.

-Connie Knighton

I missed one of the marathons at this location as I had a family event I had to attend on a lake in Muskoka over by Baysville. I showed up for the opening ceremonies, said a few words, wished them all well, and felt like hell because I had to miss the big event.

MNM #9, in 2010, had another new location: the literacy offices on the main street of town, at the north end, which had many small rooms connected by a circular hallway, which made a good place for late night wheelie chair races.

A couple of novel marathons were held there and then, in 2011, new organizers found a great new location, in a place called Club 55, on Main Street, again, in the Town Hall building, just four or five doors down from our first location.

I missed the first two in this location as I was out west, but I made it to the third event held in this place. It was a good location for many reasons. It was one big room, with air conditioning, a kitchen, bathrooms, a little room for time outs, and it was perfect for connecting with a growing event called Nuit Blanche North.

In 2013, at the 12th MNM, I made a present of my collection of press clippings, photos, invitations, awards, et cetera, relating to the marathon, to the YMCA, which had taken over from the Muskoka Literacy Council as the recipient of funds raised by the MNM, and I suggested to them that they start an archive, as it appeared the annual special event fundraiser had become an institution that would be around for a long time.

What did it mean? Why did I have a flashback to the history of the MNM?

What would happen next year?

11. Waking Up In The Zen Forest

After the driving marathon, crossing a big chunk of Canada in three days, driving ten to thirteen hours a day, and then the novel marathon, keeping ridiculous hours, writing well over 20,000 words in three days, I realized a few things.

First of all, I realized marathoners are fantastically crazy. And I mean that in the best way.

Secondly, I realized I wrote this book about driving meditation without describing driving meditation.

Thirdly, driving across Canada and then keeping crazy hours at a novel marathon is a good way to have visions. -- It might be better than meditating in the Zen Forest and going to a mukhti deeshu with a guru.

And finally, on the third day of the marathon, with half a day left, I realized that book #100 is almost finished, and it will be finished before the end of the marathon.

Maybe a note on how to write 100 books would be in order.

But first ..... Driving meditation.

At the Zen Forest, I learned and then taught simple and advanced ways to meditate. I had studied meditation in other places long before I went to the Zen Forest, of course, as I have been drawn to meditation and prayer my whole life.

Well, not my whole life.

I've had times when I've been more or less spiritual, times when I wanted to immerse myself in spirituality, and times when I've wandered away from it. I've had decades of being a kosher vegetarian, for instance, followed by a couple of years as a carnivore, eating steak and eggs for breakfast and a lot of Alberta roast beef for dinner.

Father, forgive me.

David Suzuki, please forgive me.

When I was a kid in high school in Bracebridge, I tried bio-feedback. When I took a year off school, between high school and university, I studied TM with one of the many disciples of the Maharishi Mahesh Yogi. Transcendental Meditation, as it was known, was a huge hit in North America.

The Maharishi made meditation popular in the

West by simplifying it. Before he left home with nothing much more than his simplified method of reaching nirvannah, meditation was regarded as something difficult related to yoga that required a mantra and years or decades of devotion and it was not for everyone. He told the world that meditation was for everybody and all you needed to do was study with him, or one of his students, remember your mantra, and chant a lot.

The monk and Zen master at the Zen Forest teaches a more complicated and a far simpler method.

Many people who show up at the Zen Forest, driving over from the big city, arrive with a belief that meditation is complicated. So, he gives them a complicated method for meditating. You have to sit like this, precisely, hold your hands just like this, keep the tip of your tongue just behind your teeth at the roof of your mouth, form a triangle with your tailbone and eyes and where you look at the floor in front of you, and so on and on.

The simple method, for those who can handle it, is to count your breaths.

The complicated method involves counting

breaths, from one to ten, and then starting over again, while sitting on a zafu in the zendo, for twenty minutes, to begin with, and there are a lot of Zen stories, old and new, to help you clear your mind.

The goal is hit the mute button for your brain. Most people find that very difficult.

The truth is, you should not expect your thoughts to just stop coming.

Most people get a lot of thoughts. We call that monkey mind.

I think Natalie Goldberg calls that 'wild mind'.

Picture a monkey let loose in the maple trees and white pines of your mind.

In the Zen Forest, there is a sculpture of the Buddha with children crawling all over him. If you have ever had the pleasure of having several toddlers using you as a jungle gym, you know it can get to be pretty annoying, after a time. But the Buddha is smiling.

The little kids represent your senses. Paying a lot of attention to your senses is what distracts you from meditation and clearing your mind of thoughts.

A more modern way to imagine it goes like this: Picture yourself as an air traffic controller with a big computer screen in front of you and it is your job to say which planes can land and which planes have to take off. And then treat your thoughts like that.

A lot of people have a certain set of thoughts that keep coming to mind, even while meditating, or especially while meditating, like that beautiful woman you broke up with but cannot forget, or the two dozen amazing women sitting in front of you at the novel marathon while you are trying to write your literary masterpiece.

The monk and Zen master says to treat those repetitive thoughts the way you would treat an annoying friend. Think of someone you have been friends with but you find annoying and you don't want to be around so you have developed a number of techniques for getting rid of them. Maybe you have developed a signal. When you say, I'm busy right now, they know you want them to go away for a while. You can treat your thoughts like that.

You say to yourself, oh, there's that thought about that relationship .... Well, hello there, old friend. Yes, I see you are back, I recognize you, I remember you. But I am not going with you right now or for the next twenty minutes or the next hour or the rest of the day.

Take off!

As Bob and Doug McKenzie used to say, Take off to the Great White North!

At the ZF, we invite newcomers to try sitting meditation for twenty minutes, focussed on their breathing, and then we ask them how it went.

How many times did you count your breaths, from one to ten, and then start over again.

Most people laugh nervously and say something like, I got to ten once, or I got to seven a couple of times, or, I never got past three.

With practice, you get better.

They say practice makes perfect.

Sitting practice has many benefits, but perfection is not part of the package.

After practicing sitting meditation, newcomers are taught how to do walking meditation, reclining meditation, and sleeping meditation.

They all involve breathwork, or counting breaths, or focusing on your breathing.

For walking meditation, you co-ordinate your breathing with your walking. Take a step as you breath in and take another step as you breathe out.

Try not to trip over the roots or rocks as you walk through the Zen Forest, meditating like a monk.

Reclining meditation and sleeping meditation are almost the same, except for the way you hold your head, and the fact that you keep your eyes open unless you want to fall asleep.

-- Duh!

People worry about rolling over and getting into the wrong position during sleeping meditation. People worry about a lot of things! All you have to do is get back into the proper position and then fall asleep again.

Meditating all the time, all day long, is much more complicated.

Not!

Just keep your focus on your breathing as you do all the things you do during the day.

I freaked out when the monk told me that.

I thought meditation was sacred and not something you could do while eating, having a shower, going to the bathroom, whatever.

So driving meditation is easy. While driving, while doing all the things you need to do in order to be safe, you remain conscious of your breathing, you count breaths, and you can count ten breaths and start over again or just keep your focus on your breathing.

It reminds me of the Jesus prayer, described by J.D. Salinger in Franny And Zooey, a novel we all read while in high school.

Praying constantly is the theme at the heart of Franny and Zooey. It is Franny who learns the Jesus Prayer from the religious "Pilgrim" books.

By incessantly praying to Jesus, the person who prays is endowed with "Christ-Consciousness," in Zooey's words, and can see God, in Franny's words.

What Franny realizes only at the end of the novel, spoiler alert, is that not only does one unite with Jesus through the prayer, but through all humanity, since everyone carries Christ within him or herself.

The Jesus Prayer has more to do with love than with religion, as incessant praying spans several religions.

The Jesus Prayer, or "The Prayer", or "The Wish" is a short, prayer that goes like this: Lord Jesus Christ, Son of God, have mercy on me, the sinner.

There are a few versions of the Jesus Prayer. Some people say, Lord Jesus Christ, Son of God, have mercy on me. Or Lord Jesus Christ, have mercy on me.

Jesus, have mercy.

Lord Jesus Christ, Son of God, have mercy on us.

Lord Jesus Christ, Son of the living God, have mercy on me, a sinner.

Some people use prayer beads to help them pray incessantly.

Buddhist prayer beads are a traditional tool used to count the number of times a mantra is recited while meditating. They are similar to other forms of prayer beads used in various world religions.

My favourite way to pray is with a prayer shawl over my head, rocking gently, or bobbing and weaving, or shuckling, or shokeling, from the

Yiddish word meaning "to shake".

Shokeling is the ritual swaying during Jewish prayer, usually forward and back, but also from side to side.

That practice can be traced back as far Talmudic times, they say, and it is believed that it increases concentration and emotional intensity.

The Singing Rabbi said that, in Chassidic lore, shuckeling is seen as an expression of the soul's desire to abandon the body and reunite itself with its source, similar to a flame's shaking back and forth as if to free itself from the wick.

They say the Talmud has existed forever and before it was written with black ink on white paper it existed in the form of black fire on white fire.

However, shokeling while driving can be a little difficult, and wearing a prayer shawl over your head, while driving, presents obvious problems.

Using prayer beads while driving can cause problems, too. There is a great scene in the Jim Carrey movie called Bruce Almighty that shows a car crash while he's talking to God and using prayer beads.

However, it is not difficult to think about your breathing, or count breaths, while driving, even you don't have automatic transmission, and it doesn't matter if you stop counting while you deal with difficult situations, like closed lanes in the traffic circle around Saskatoon, heading east, or Winnipeg, heading west, or places with awe-inspiring, breath-taking, views, like most of the route north of Superior.

So .... That's how you do it. Drive and breathe.

That's my big message for this book: Don't forget to breathe.

The monk and Zen master says, smartly, If you aren't breathing, you aren't living.

-- No kidding!

It's important to stay awake while driving, obviously. They say driving tired is worse than driving drunk. There are lots of signs along the Trans-Canada Highway saying Fatigue Kills / Take A Break.

Staying awake in the spiritual sense is another matter.

Waking up is hard to do, they say.

Breaking up is hard to do, the song says.

Waking up, or having an enlightenment experience, is not really that rare. But staying awake is something else.

Jesus said, Keep awake! numerous times.

The Zen master in the Zen Forest often says, Wake up! or You have to wake up! or Try to wake up before you drop dead!

Deepak Chopra says there are several levels of consciousness. Every spiritual tradition speaks of higher states of consciousness and Deepak Chopra says it is especially in the Vedanta that we find such a structured map of these stages of development.

The average person only experiences three states of consciousness in an entire lifetime, they say. These are deep sleep, dreams, and waking state of consciousness.

Spiritual practice or sadhana begins the process by which an individual transforms his or her consciousness from these three common states of consciousness into " higher states" of consciousness.

Any of the four primary yoga practices (the yogas of being, feeling, thinking, doing) the mind is led past its conditioned states to its pure unconditioned state.

Beyond the first 3 states of consciousness are the following four states: Soul consciousness, Cosmic consciousness, Divine consciousness and Unity consciousness.

Soul consciousness is the state we experience when we shift from body, mind, and ego, to the observer of the body, mind, and ego. We experience and cultivate Soul consciousness when we meditate.

This observer is referred to as the witnessing awareness. During meditation, a person begins to identify with this aspect of the Self which is beyond thinking and feeling, (the silent witness), and then he or she begins to feel more calm, centered and intuitive in daily life.

As the authentic core of oneself solidifies, there is less emotional drama in their lives. Relationships are more loving and compassionate and one finds a deeper, more caring relationship with the environment and nature.

Meditation has been shown to lead to the

reduction of stress markers, slower heart rate, lower blood pressure, enhanced immune function, and so on. People who practice meditation are less prone to sickness.

Cosmic consciousness is the state when soul consciousness gets stabilized and the witnessing awareness is present all the time in waking, dreaming, and sleeping states.

In the Christian tradition the phrase "to be in the world and not of it," describes this flavor of Cosmic consciousness.

In this state, even during deep sleep, the witnessing awareness is fully awake and there is the realization that one is not the mind/body, which is in the field of change, but rather an eternal spirit that transcends space and time.

The most remarkable aspect of this state of consciousness is the knowledge of one's nature as timeless and therefore no fear of death.

Cosmic consciousness is not the pinnacle of enlightenment, but it marks the critical transition from an identity bound to a conditioned life, to a life of freedom in self-knowledge.

Divine consciousness is the expansion of cosmic consciousness.

The ever-present witnessing awareness is experienced and dormant abilities such as the awakening of the non-local senses (referred to in Sanskrit as tanmatras) begin to be experienced.

As the individual mind starts to access these unused realms of the psyche, they will activate extraordinary spiritual abilities previously thought to be unattainable, including experiences such as knowledge of past and future, clairvoyance, a refined sense of taste, smell, sight, touch and hearing, control over bodily functions, heart rate, and autonomic functions, et cetera.

In other words, objects are experienced simultaneously on the sensory level and a subtle, more abstract, level.

Appreciation of life from this more refined perspective represents the real engagement of the heart and love as the engine of spiritual growth at this stage, they say. By experiencing the patterns and deeper connections that underlie external diversity, we find our soul is stirred by a profound sense of beauty, awe, compassion, gratitude and love.

In Divine Consciousness, this harmonizing and synthesizing power is felt as the presence of Divinity in our heart. Wherever one goes, one feels the presence of the Divine.

Vedic seers would say that in Divine consciousness, God is not difficult to find, but impossible to avoid.

At this stage, there is an even greater conviction of the immortality of existence, not only as nonlocal consciousness, but also in the knowledge that you are that enduring presence of divine love.

Divine consciousness also brings a deeper experience of liberation, as the external sensory world is no longer seen as a kind of spiritual exile which the soul must endure, but rather the world is a manifestation of the beauty, and love of one's consciousness and therefore integral to one's spirituality.

Unity consciousness is also referred to as Brahman consciousness. It is a state of consciousness where the ever-present witness is not just recognized as the core of one's existence, but it is perceived as the primary reality of every experience.

The culmination of enlightenment, according to some, is the knowledge that consciousness alone exists, that is all there is , was, or ever will be.

That oneness, or unity, dominates awareness even as one engages in the same mundane details of life as before, such as driving a car, or doing all the things you usually do.

You no longer identify with an individual body-mind apparatus, you see the whole universe as your physical body.

And that's why we meditate all day long, while doing other things, such as driving across Canada. And that's why we keep working on reaching higher stages of enlightenment, even when we are surrounded by devas and we are in heaven, as we are at the novel marathon.

Everyone wakes up at their speed or pace or time. It could happen just before you die. It could happen fast. You might wake up then fall asleep then wake up for a longer period of time, then fall asleep, then wake up again .... This is called kensho.

Some people work hard at meditating, try really hard, day after day. This doesn't help! You will wake up when you wake up. You might get a glimpse of what it's like in a peak moment, such as while skiing, or contemplating a sunrise, or seeing the first robin of spring, or sitting in a Muskoka chair on a dock by lake until a water skier splashes you.

A few years ago, I spent three days meditating at Omega Holistic Institute near Woodstock while listening to Deepak Chopra identify the seven levels of awareness or conscsiousness or waking up, which is the goal of meditation. He said most people on the planet experience only three levels of awareness: being awake, sleeping, and dreaming. So those are the first 3 levels. The 4th level is soul consciousness. W.O. Mitchell called this the extra-spectator quality and said all artists have this. Deepak says, You are listening to me now, but just turn your awareness to who is listening, while you are listening, and you will glimpse your soul. That kind of awareness is soul consciousness.

There's a great video about this, called "Dude, Check out my new karma," on Youtube.

Levels 5, 6, and 7, are cosmic, unity, and divine. Cosmic consciousness is what Christians call Christ consciousness. Or as Jesus said, You are in the world but not of the world. At this level, Deepak Chopra says, you don't have to go looking for God, because you can't help running into God wherever you go, wherever you look you see God.

There is a song I like that reminds me of this: Victor Wooten's "I Saw God".

Unity consciousness means your feel connected to everything. We joke about this. What did the Zen master say when he went to pizza pizza? Make me one with everything. But we have all had moments when we feel in the zone and connected to everything and it's all good.

And divine consciousness, Deepak Chopra says, is when you realize you are God. And in this state, it is the best time for manifesting, using the law of attraction, but don't waste it on getting the best parking spot or a lottery ticket. Ask for the highest guidance and to be part of the evolutionary flow of the universe.

I have never experienced this, but sometimes I feel like I'm getting there when I listen to the Moola Mantra, by Deva Premal.

But, this is not Zen. But Zen can help you experience those states, if that's what you believe in. Zen is the tool that helps you experience those states of consciousness.

At the Zen Forest, we don't talk about seven levels, we talk about three: are you awake or asleep and if you have woken up can you stay awake and reach nirvana or enlightenment. That's it. Zen means simple.

So, try to meditate all the time. Reading -- even speed reading. Writing, too. At a concert, a movie, a workshop on Zen, add Zen. Meditate while at the concert or the movie or the workshop. Focus on your breathing, and take it in.

Say you go to a poetry reading. Zen can deepen your appreciation of the poetry, if you meditate while listening.

Writing practice can be Zen. Natalie Goldberg promotes this idea. And before her, W.O. Mitchell and Ray Bradbury promoted this idea. Goldberg's book, Wild Mind, is like Bradbury's book, Zen In The Art Of Writing. W.O. Mitchell didn't write a book about writing, but he taught writing, and he taught us MMM, which is writing without thinking. Freefall, freewriting, the write/write method. You empty your mind onto paper.

Try this: Follow Zen meditation with Zen massage and then Zen Qigong. That's the key, the triple play, the hat-trick!

P.S. The Zen Monk says, If you are not working on enlightenment, you may as well watch hockey on TV.

This is the Zen Forest short-cut to enlightenment. It's a big secret or tip or revelation. It's good to meditate 20 minutes around sunrise or sunset, but you have 24 hours a day available to you. Meditate all the time and add Zen to whatever you do.

So, the question is, What does enlightenment look like? How will we know when we get there?

So let me ask you: What is nirvana, or enlightenment? What does it look like? How will we know when we get there? Let me ask you: What is your conception of enlightenment.

I asked a Zen Master and a New Age Guru this question.

The New Age Guru said, imagine, envision, visualize in 3D, using all your senses, heaven on Earth, and how you would be introduced if you were at the top level of consciousness and realized you are God.

The Zen Master said, for our next book, we could look at Buddhist heaven and hell. The different levels of reincarnation: animal, human, heaven with divas, hell, hungry ghosts, jealousy and war.

He said, we could write a book about the

levels of hell, the 8 cold Narakas and the 8 Hot Narakas. Some say there are 500 Buddhist hells. Some say there are thousands.

The worst hell description came from China during the Communist Revolution: you walk through a forest, leaves fall like razor blades, slicing and dicing you, but you come together again, walk through a forest, and the same thing happens again and again for thousands of years.

Imagine paper cuts, mosquitoes and blackflies, horseflies, over and over.

But, the Zen master says, nobody has to read that book. They just have to read the book Wake Up Here And New: How To Recover Your Life Before It's Over, or How To Die Laughing, because:

1. Nobody has died and reported on it
2. those levels of heaven and hell are states of mind, here and now. This is heaven. And this is hell. So, take the Zen Forest short-cut, get out of hell, and go to heaven. That's it! Wake up!

Who would have thought that the highest enlightenment, attributed to Christ and Buddha, is just who you are?!

Human beings are both good and evil; enlightenment is within their grasp, yet most are blinded and consumed by their desires.

The realm of heavenly beings filled with pleasure; the deva hold godlike powers; most live in delightful happiness and splendor; they live for countless ages, but even the Deva belong to the world of suffering (samsara) -- for their powers blind them to the world of suffering and fill them with pride

The goal is to end karma and get off the cycle or rebirth. What's that like? Energy floating around the universe, they say.

After you deepen your meditation with Zen, some people develop their healing abilities with Zen. So, Quantum Touch becomes Zen Quantum Touch, Reiki becomes Zen Reiki, Energy Healing with Qigong becomes Zen Qigong Energy Healing. Deepak Chopra says this is the kind of healing Jesus did, and that he learned it in India, during his "Lost Years". And anybody can do it. Some people develop their abilities more than others.

As the 2013 Muskoka Novel Marathon ends, I am in the moment, finishing book #100, called Long Quiet Canadian Highway: Waking Up In Canada, but I am thinking of the other novel marathons I've been in, and my life in Alberta, and before that, and I am thinking of the near future, as well. Soon I will have a reunion with my brother and we will go swimming, canoeing, and kayaking, possibly, in the warm water where he lives. He loves Balm Beach on Georgian Bay.

And after that, I will head down to the Zen Forest. I'll drive from Georgian Bay to Lake Ontario, again, through Central Ontario, going from Coldwater through Muskoka, Haliburton, Peterborough, and along the Trans-Canada Highway, again, to the country north of Belleville, as the poet Al Purdy said, to visit the monk and Zen master again.

It would be faster to get on Highway 400 and The 401, but they are the opposite of quiet highways. The TCH through Central Ontario, to the Zen Forest, is another piece of the long, quiet,

Canadian highway.

Later I will re-connect with the New Age guru, and ask her what she thinks of the new vision I've had, with so many female spiritual leaders looking at me, with their little Mona Lisa smiles.

I'm left wondering if or when my two big visions, or enlightenment moments, or near-death experiences, will come together. First I saw Jesus, Buddha, Bodhidharma, and the boys, and then I saw the "female Jesus", Venerable Dhyani Ywahoo, Margot Anand, and the girls.

I know what you're thinking: Why can't they all get together?

Maybe I'll find out when I get to a higher level of enlightenment.

I'll let you know.

12. Waking Up At Balm Beach

The morning after Muskoka Novel Marathon #12, I woke up up in Arrowhead Provincial Park, in my tent, at sunrise, when the birds were making their morning racket. I felt a little tired after writing a novel in 3 days after driving across half of Canada in 3 days after packing up to move for 3 days. The first thing I wanted to do was go for a swim.

There is nothing like an early morning swim in a little lake up north in Canada.

Northern Muskoka did not feel as though it was "north", any more, since I had spent the past two years in Northern Alberta.

I marveled at all the trees and wildflowers in the park and the great increase in bio-diversity as I traveled from the 55th parallel to the 45th parallel. There was more of everything, the further south I went.

After swimming across Arrowhead Lake, and back, I went to town for breakfast, for Buddha's Bowl at Soul Sista's Wellness Cafe.

I checked my e-mail in the cafe, since they had

free wifi, and saw a growing list of accolades from the people at the novel marathon.

Everybody made it home safely, after the marathon, and went on Facebook to say MNM #12 was a big hit.

From there, I drove down to Port Sydney, to see the natural water slide between Mary Lake and the Muskoka River.

I made a quick stop at High Falls, after that, formerly known as Niagara of the North. There is a good place to swim a little downriver from the big waterfall.

Bracebridge was next on my list: the town where I lived, a decade earlier, and where I went to high school, before that. I was shocked to see they were tearing down the old high school building. All the new section, at the back, was already down, and left in a big pile of rubble, but the oldest part, at the front, was left standing.

I was happy to see that Bracebridge Falls was still roaring.

Around the time I left, there was a controversy over using in-stream technology to get more hydro-electric power out of the falls, even though it would reduce the flow of water over the scenic waterfall.

The North Branch of the Muskoka River looked great, but I didn't swim there. I had a strong desire to go to Muskoka Beach.

I drove down to Gravenhurst and went for a swim at my favourite beach before cruising through town to see the new building at the Bethune House, the old building which was the house I grew up in, the main street, and Gull Lake Park.

Everything looked new and terrific except the house of my childhood. It had not changed at all in the decades since I lived there.

That's almost four decades without any changes to the exterior or to the property.

Muskoka Beach looked the same, too, but in this case the lack of change was a very good thing. It was still a well-kept secret, apparently, as there was almost nobody there, despite the fact it is a great place to go for a swim.

Muskoka Beach is a public beach on Lake Muskoka, and there aren't many of those. It is a sandy beach in a rocky part of the country. The hard-packed, golden sand, without boulders, rocks, or stones, under clear water, looks beautiful. The bay beside the Hoc Roc River, across from Muskoka Sands Inn, now called Taboo, is shallow, so the water is warm.

It remains shallow for a long way out. You can walk for about one hundred yards before it is over your head and then it only drops to about ten feet deep. The water is shallow like that all the way out to the first group of islands, and then drops off steeply to deep water.

The big bay with the warm, blue water looks beautiful and it felt fantastic to walk into it.

The water temperature wasn't much different than the air temperature.

After that, Gull Lake looked like a great big glacial pot hole, or a little lake in Norway.

I kept driving south, through Muskoka, and noticed South Muskoka was still the roughest looking part of the district, from the south end of Gravenhurst to the big rock cut at Severn Bridge and the bridge over the Severn River, which marks the end of Muskoka and the Canadian Shield.

I went a little further south, to Orillia, and then

got on the Trans-Canada Highway, to go to Midland, and then headed over to Penetanguishine, where my brother lives, past Martyr's Shrine, and through Penetang to the country, near Awenda Provincial Park, where my brother lives.

We went to Balm Beach, later that afternoon, after talking for a while, and swam in Georgian Bay. We kept on going in the water and getting out to get heated up on the beach and then going back in the water again.

My brother lives in Tiny township, near Penetang and Midland, in the southern Georgian Bay region, and it comprises the communities of Allenwood Beach, Ardmore Beach, Balm Beach, Belle-Eau-Claire Beach, Bluewater Beach, Cawaja Beach, Cedar Point, Clearwater Beach, Cove Beach, Crescent Beach, Coutenac Beach, Deanlea Beach, Edmore Beach, Georgian Sands Beach, Georgina Beach, Gibson, Ishpiming Beach, Kettle's Beach, Lafontaine Beach, Mountain View Beach, Nottawaga Beach, Ossossane Beach, Rowntree Beach, Sandcastle Beach, Sandy Bay, Silver Birch Beach, Thunder Beach, Tiny Beach, Wahnekewaning Beach, Wendake Beach,

Woodland Beach, and Wymbolwood Beach, as well as a few other tiny places.

Balm Beach is linked to Wasaga Beach, which is the longest freshwater beach in the world. Wasaga Beach Provincial Park is the first provincial park in Canada awarded the Blue Flag designation for its efforts to manage Wasaga's shoreline according to international environmental standards. Wikipedia says over two million people visit the town every summer to stroll the shores of the Wasaga's freshwater beach (stretching 14 kilometres or 8.7 miles), swim in warm clean waters, and enjoy the panoramic mountain views across the bay.

Balm Beach was heavenly. It was a real balm.

If you dove down to the bottom, when it was about six feet deep, the water was cold, and refreshing, but close to the surface it was almost as warm as the water at Muskoka Beach.

My brother is still a strong swimmer, in his seventies, so we swam quite far out, together, and back again.

I spent a lot of time floating on my back, relaxing my spine, looking at the Blue Mountains in the distance, and the blue sky above, meditating Zen Forest style, in heaven, surrounded by devas, working on enlightenment, and thinking about the New Age guru's advice: rest and re-group in July.

And I hadn't forgotten the promise about new energies and opportunities appearing in the autumn. It was going to be a time when it would become possible to do do what was formerly unimaginable.

My summer of resting and re-grouping got off to a great start, saying "so long" to Alberta and the Rocky Mountains, driving from the Rockies to the longest freshwater beach in the world, followed by the novel marathon and a swimming marathon. It's a big country, this place we call home, and it has a long, quiet, Canadian highway, perfect for driving meditation, from coast to coast, and every day of the trip you can wake up in Canada.